NEW TESTAMENT

2 PETER AND JUDE

2 PETER AND JUDE

Jonathan Knight

Sheffield Academic Press

Copyright © 1995 Sheffield Academic Press

Published by Sheffield Academic Press Ltd
Mansion House
19 Kingfield Road
Sheffield, S11 9AS
England

Printed on acid-free paper in Great Britain
by The Cromwell Press
Melksham, Wiltshire

British Library Cataloguing in Publication Data

A catalogue record for this book is available
from the British Library

ISBN 1-85075-744-5

Contents

Abbreviations 7

1. Introduction 9
2. Reading Jude 37
3. Reading 2 Peter 57
4. Jude and 2 Peter in the Context of Early
   Christianity 75

Bibliography 87
Index of References 90
Index of Authors 94

Abbreviations

AB	Anchor Bible
JBL	*Journal of Biblical Literature*
JSJ	*Journal for the Study of Judaism in the Persian, Hellenistic and Roman Period*
JTS	*Journal of Theological Studies*
NCB	New Century Bible
SBLDS	SBL Dissertation Series
SBT	Studies in Biblical Theology
ZNW	*Zeitschrift für die neutestamentliche Wissenschaft*

1
INTRODUCTION

New Testament literature for most readers falls into a number of categories. There is material that we have all known from childhood like the infancy narratives in the Gospels and some of the stories in Acts. Secondly, passages of acknowledged importance such as Paul's letter to the Romans, the eighth chapter in particular, and John's Gospel. Thirdly, books which seem important but which are also difficult and which therefore seem daunting; Revelation and Hebrews are examples of these. Finally, works which are seldom read and whose contents generally remain unfamiliar. Into this last category fall the two subjects of this volume, Jude and 2 Peter. Both texts have often been outshone by other documents and sometimes been regarded (as during the Reformation) as of scant importance. Neither of them is easy to understand. Their language is sometimes difficult, and the symbolism and biblical allusions, especially in Jude, obscure to readers who do not know Jewish apocalyptic literature. Both, however, stand in the Canon and for that reason deserve as much attention as better known documents if we are to achieve a balanced understanding of the New Testament and its major concerns. The letters in fact repay careful study. They reveal a thought world that is dominated by meditation on biblical literature, and they show how such material was interpreted to deal with problems in the life of certain (unknown) early churches in the mid- to late-first century CE.

Why Read Jude and 2 Peter Together?

At first sight it might appear that Jude and 2 Peter are taken together in this Guide as a convenient way of dealing with material that seems difficult to date and to exegete. This is not a full assessment of the issue. The two texts are generally treated together (as they are here) because, according to the best results of research, one of them makes use of the other. The amount of material which they hold in common makes this conclusion almost inevitable. While a 'common source' theory has occasionally been canvassed, the general consensus of opinion is that the author of 2 Peter used Jude and that his letter represents an early exegesis of that text. This is the view which is accepted in this Guide.

The association between Jude and 2 Peter thus draws on the results of literary criticism. We can find examples elsewhere in the New Testament of one author using the work of another—the use of Pauline literature by the writer of Ephesians is an example of this—but 2 Peter's use of Jude is more substantial. The author of 2 Peter incorporates much of Jude in his letter although he makes certain modifications which are designed to support his own argument. This is not just influence by an earlier author but the deliberate and extensive use of an earlier text, probably one that had become widely known in Christian churches, to undergird a message which this later writer wished to convey.

This conclusion has important consequences for discussion of the authorship and date of 2 Peter. Despite the claim that Peter wrote the letter it seems unlikely that this was so. 2 Peter is rather pseudonymous: it is a work that claims to be by the apostle but which was really written by a later author who used the fiction of apostolic authorship to gain authority for what he said. The suggestion of pseudepigraphy should occasion neither suspicion nor surprise for readers of the New Testament. In Paul's collection of writings Ephesians is almost certainly not by the apostle and doubts have been raised about Colossians, 2 Thessalonians and the Pastorals as well. Pseudepigraphy is in fact a recurrent feature of New Testament literature, especially of the later documents. The author of 2 Peter did not set out to deceive his readers by

1. Introduction

doing this. They would almost certainly have known where the letter came from. He rather wanted to gain support for his rejection of false teaching by claiming the persona of Peter, the apostle and confidant of the Lord (just as he used Jude and refers also to the Hebrew Scriptures and to Paul). There is a possibility that Jude is also pseudonymous, but this is much less certain than in the case of 2 Peter.

Approaching the Material: Jude

Before matters of dating and authorship are examined, it will be helpful to glance through the two texts and to explain what they contain. Jude will be addressed before 2 Peter since the view taken here is that that 2 Peter is later and partly dependent on it.

Jude claims to be from Jude, the brother of James (v. 1). This James is doubtless James the Just, the brother also of Jesus, whom we know from Acts to have been the leader of the primitive church in Jerusalem (Acts 12.17; 15.13-21; cf. Gal. 2.11-14). Of all the James' in the New Testament (e.g. James the brother of John; and James the son of Alphaeus mentioned by Mt. 10.3) he is the most likely candidate. This identification makes Jude, too, the brother of Jesus, although other Judes have sometimes been proposed (see below) and we have yet to consider the issue of pseudonymity.

Jude has the form of a letter. That is to say, it has an introduction (v. 1), a salutation (vv. 1-2), a body (vv. 3-23) and a conclusion (vv. 24-25). Despite attempts to present it as a 'catholic' or 'general' epistle, one that was written to address a variety of false teaching in many churches, it seems more likely that Jude was addressed to a specific situation. The letter's brevity is an indication that this was so. As we shall see, that situation was dominated by the readers' experience of false teachers: people who had an antinomian or libertine strand to their message. Charles (1993, ch. 2) examines the letter's affinities with what he calls the 'word of exhortation' discourse, a Jewish and Christian form of writing which used earlier examples to recommend a particular pattern of behaviour to readers. This theory perhaps supports the view that Jude was addressed to a specific rather than to a general situation.

Jude begins with a traditional form of address (v. 1). The recipients are described as 'those who have been called', those 'loved by God the Father and kept by Jesus Christ'. This makes it difficult to reconstruct their identity. Despite our curiosity, we can only now say that they would have known who they were! Some manuscripts add the phrase 'to the Gentiles' in v. 1 but this is not supported by the better manuscripts, and it seems more likely from the nature of the scriptural allusions that the recipients would have had a Jewish background (although the church may have been in a Gentile area and thus have included Gentiles). It is possible that Jude was addressed to more than one church but we have no certain way of commenting on the identity and the circumstances of the recipients.

The author's purpose in writing can be discerned from vv. 3-4 (cf. also vv. 17-23). These verses show that the letter was written to provide exhortation to readers who were troubled by false teachers. Certain people had apparently infiltrated the readers' community and begun to do what Jude calls 'perverting the grace of our God into licentiousness, and denying our only Master and Lord, Jesus Christ' (v. 4). This passage reveals that the troublemakers had come from outside and that they taught a licentious gospel. Perhaps this involved the suggestion of antinomianism, the idea that it is possible to live without the rule of law. This was an issue which had troubled some of the Pauline churches (see Gal. 5.13; 1 Cor. 6.12). Later in Jude it appears that the liberal teaching had a sexual orientation (v. 7) and it may have involved sponging on community hospitality as well (v. 12). The author wrote to warn readers about the dangers of those who advocated these kind of practices and he used the familiar biblical language of judgment to do this.

Verse 5 introduces a series of scriptural examples on the theme of judgment. These are designed to show the error of what the teachers were saying and to present them in the same terms as notorious biblical sinners. The author mentions the Exodus (v. 5), the story of the Fallen Watchers in Genesis 6 (v. 6), and the Sodom and Gomorrah story (v. 7). In each case the use made of these stories is a typological one. That is to say, Jude presents the Old Testament events as a

1. *Introduction*

warning for contemporary sinners, which makes the point that their fate had been foretold in earlier history. Readers are shown through a chain of examples that judgment inexorably followed sin. The argument is based on the belief that there was no difference between what had happened in the past and the contemporary situation in this regard. This use of Scripture can be compared with Paul's statement in 1 Cor. 10.11 that the Mosaic writings contained information that worked for the benefit of Christians as members of the eschatological generation.

Verse 8 describes the teachers' activity in more detail. The author says that they were polluting their bodies, rejecting authority, and slandering celestial beings. This confirms that the problem had a sexual dimension. Verse 9 introduces an apocryphal story about Michael which shows the meaning of the slander reference. It tells how the archangel, when he disputed with the devil for the body of Moses, did not bring a slanderous accusation against him but said only, 'The Lord rebuke you!'. This allusion criticizes those who slandered angels, apparently by denying their authority as guardians of the Law, by citing the example of the angel chief who refused to do this. This tends to confirm that the teachers had suggested that the Jewish Law was redundant. Verse 10 then says that they spoke abusively against things they did not understand (again, apparently the importance of angels in mediating the Law) and that they followed their animal passions, for which reason they incurred judgment.

Verse 11 introduces three false teachers from Jewish tradition: Cain, Balaam and Korah. This reference depends for its effect on Jewish interpretation of the Bible, where all three of these enticed others to sin. Again, this material is designed to show the false teachers in their true colours as people who led others astray. According to v. 12 they were blemishes at the Christian love feasts, at which they caroused and fed only themselves. They were feckless people (described under a variety of images) for whom the nether darkness (clearly that of punishment or destruction) had been reserved (v. 13).

Jude 14 introduces a citation from *1 En.* 1.9. This text had anticipated that God would come from heaven with his angels to execute judgment. The author of Jude refers it to the *parousia* of Jesus and assumes (in common with all first-century Christians) that Jesus would return from heaven as the Lord to punish those who acted immorally. The citation from *1 Enoch* is followed by further criticism of the teachers as grumblers, fault finders, and impassioned boasters who flattered others for the advantage which it gave them (v. 16).

Verses 17-18 brings us to the heart of the letter. Jude there introduces some words of the apostles whom it is claimed had foretold the rise of 'scoffers' in what are called 'the last days'. 'Scoffers' are defined here as 'people who follow their own ungodly passions'. Three statements are made about these 'scoffers' in v. 19: they had divided the community, they followed their natural instincts, and they lacked the Holy Spirit. In contrast readers were told to build themselves up in the faith (a request which in this context has ethical implications) and to pray in the Holy Spirit (v. 20). They must keep themselves in God's love as they waited for the mercy of the Lord Jesus to bring them to eternal life (v. 21).

Verses 22-23a have suffered textual corruption and this makes them difficult to interpret. Verse 22 advocates mercy towards those who doubted (or disputed?). These are evidently the teachers and probably also those who were tempted to follow them. Verse 23 introduces the image of fire from Zech. 3.2 to describe their perilous position. Not even the clothing which they wore was to be tolerated (v. 23c)—a strong comment on the need for separateness and moral purity.

The benediction and doxology in vv. 24-25 affirm the common Christian eschatological hope. The author anticipated the *parousia*, the return of Jesus from heaven, and insisted that everyone must appear before God at the end so that the theme of judgment is by implication reiterated (cf. vv. 14-15). The author says that God was able to keep them from falling—in other words, he would help them resist the false teachers—and that he would bring them blameless through the present crisis. For this reason, the letter concludes, he must be glorified through Jesus for ever.

1. Introduction

Approaching the Material: 2 Peter

2 Peter was written after Jude and shows a knowledge of that letter. Like Jude 2 Peter is also addressed to a situation that was dominated by what the author held to be inappropriate teaching. His use of Jude reveals certain features of that situation, notably its libertine or antinomian aspect, but this should not be taken to imply that the situation was identical in every respect. Chapter 3 contains evidence for an eschatological disillusionment on the part of those whom he criticized as well as for antinomian tendencies (cf. also 1.16-18). Confusion between the situations addressed by the two documents has been perhaps the greatest fault of research into Jude and 2 Peter this century.

The difference from Jude lies in the fact that the teachers opposed by 2 Peter had evidently denied the Christian belief in the *parousia* and future cosmic destruction (3.4). Neyrey (1980) has noted the similarities between this world-view and the ideas of Epicurean philosophy, which denied the validity of belief in providence and retribution (see also his 1993: 122-28). Epicurean beliefs had penetrated Jewish circles by the early Common Era (see e.g. the Palestinian Targums of Gen. 4.8) and Neyrey's presentation of 2 Peter's false teachers in this light seems a good explanation of their identity. They may not themselves have been Epicureans but they had conceivably been influenced by Epicurean ideas. The first readers of 2 Peter were probably Gentile Christians, people who would not have understood all the scriptural allusions made by Jude 11 which this author carefully edited (see e.g. 2 Pet. 2.15-16), but who may have known something about popular philosophy and have been able to produce arguments for denying the relevance of belief in the return of Jesus and in subsequent judgment.

2 Peter incorporates two literary genres. It is on the face of it a letter, probably one that was sent by the Roman Church to another congregation which was causing concern. It also incorporates material appropriate to the Jewish literary genre called the 'Testament'. The 'Testament' was the last speech of a dying person in which he imparted information about the future combined with ethical admonition (see

further Kolenkow 1975). There are many examples of the Testament in Jewish literature and the genre is of essence pseudonymous. Most examples are associated with heroes of old; Abraham and Moses are two such figures. 2 Peter preserves the traditional pseudepigraphy but significantly claims to present the Testament of a person who had only recently died. Peter apparently died in the Neronian Persecution of 64 CE (see Ignatius, *Rom.* 4.3; *1 Clem.* 5.4; and *Asc. Isa.* 4.3). This reformulation of the testamentary genre reflected Peter's acquaintance with Jesus and the fact that Christianity represented the final divine revelation in the author's view. His adoption of Peter's persona was first and foremost an attempt to gain authority. This use of the testamentary genre makes 2 Peter perhaps the clearest example of pseudepigraphy in the New Testament.

After the usual introduction and salutation (1.1-2) 1.3-11 presents a summary of the author's message. The letter opens with the hint that all was not well (1.3-4). The author says that God had supplied everything needed for life and godliness, and that He had enabled people to share the divine nature and to escape the corruption that existed in the world through evil desires (1.3-4). The community addressed was thus evidently one that had been tempted by 'evil desires', sexual desires no doubt included. They were reminded of the need for godly living which is exemplified by a catalogue of virtues (1.5-8). The author asserts that those who failed to display these virtues were blind and had forgotten that they had been cleansed from sins in the past (1.9). This gives a strong indication that ethical problems featured in the situation addressed by the author. The command to 'make your calling and election sure' (1.10) is as much a call to right behaviour as it is to unwavering trust and belief. 1.11 emphasizes the theme of eschatological reward, which is significant in view of the evident temptation to waver, and offers assurance that those who lived good lives would be welcomed into Christ's eternal kingdom.

1.12-18 reinforces the fiction that Peter was the writer by alluding to his impending death. This passage makes the occasion for the letter Peter's desire that people would remember his teaching once he was dead (1.15). 1.16-18

1. Introduction

mentions the Transfiguration, when Jesus had appeared to the disciples in the garments of a heavenly being (cf. Mk 9.1-8 and parallels). Surprisingly this is the only reference to that event in the New Testament outside the Synoptic Gospels. It is included here because the author saw the Transfiguration as anticipatory of the *parousia* of Jesus, which the opponents were denying and which was a belief that he wanted the readers to retain. Peter's vision of the transformed Jesus is made part of the authority for what is said in the letter about future judgment. The witness of Scripture ('prophecy') is cited as a further guarantee of truth on this matter (1.19-21). This second witness would last until the 'day dawned' and the 'morning star appeared'. Both of these are images of the *parousia*.

This reference to prophecy introduces the main theme which is the appearance of false teachers in the church (2.1ff.). These were expected to introduce 'destructive heresies' (2.1). The main part of ch. 2 emphasizes that those who did this would be punished. This is demonstrated by a catena of examples from Jewish tradition which are mainly based on Jude. 2 Pet. 2.4 alludes to the fate of the Watchers, that of imprisonment in dungeons prior to judgment. 2.5 introduces a reference to Noah, which is not found in Jude and which was possibly suggested by a Jewish source, and describes the Flood as an example of judgment. 2.6 cites the example of Sodom and Gomorrah and makes this a further type of what would happen to the ungodly. God's rescue of the righteous Lot (2.7-8), who was distressed at the behaviour that he saw around him, is then held to illustrate how God would rescue the godly while holding the unrighteous under punishment.

This passage is followed by a broader description of what the teachers were doing (2.10-22). These people are held to be bold and arrogant and they were not afraid to slander celestial beings from which even angels demurred (2.10-11). They blasphemed in matters which they did not understand and they acted like brute beasts by following their instincts (2.12). 2.13 says that they liked to carouse in daylight and that they revelled in their dissipation. Their eyes were full of adultery, they seduced the unstable, and they were experts in greed (2.14). 2.15 picks up the reference to Balaam (but not to Cain or Korah) from Jude 11. Balaam is said to have loved the wages of wickedness but to have been rebuked for this by his donkey (2.15-16). 2.17-18 states that the teachers were springs without water and mists driven by the storm (2.17). They mouthed empty words and enticed the vulnerable by appealing to lustful desires (2.18). 2.19 evidently reveals something of their message: they promised people 'freedom' but the author believes that they themselves were slaves to depravity. He says that, after escaping the world's corruption through knowing Jesus but then having reimmersed themselves in corruption, they were now worse off than before (2.20, cf. Mt. 12.45). It was better for them never to have known the way of righteousness than to turn their backs on it (2.21). Two sayings, one of them from Proverbs, are cited to confirm the folly of this behaviour (2.22): the dog returning to its vomit, and the clean sow returning to the mud.

Chapter 3 develops the suggestion of Petrine authorship to deal with the issue of the *parousia* and judgment. The author says that this was now the second letter that he had written to the readers (3.1). This suggests that he knew 1 Peter and the view taken here is that this comment is intended to reinforce the pseudepigraphy. The issue of scepticism about the *parousia* is introduced by the statement that the apostles had predicted the appearance of scoffers who asked, 'Where is the promise of his coming?' (3.3-4). These people are reported to have complained that things continued as they always had done even though the original Christian generation ('the fathers') had died (3.4). There is a similar statement in *1 Clement* 23 but we should not necesssarily question the historicity of this report for that reason. Perhaps these peoples' scepticism was partly based on the saying, which is attributed to Jesus in Mk 9.1, that some of the original disciples would not taste death until they had seen the kingdom's powerful arrival (see further Chapter 4 of this Guide). Though the point should not be exaggerated, belief about the plausibility of the *parousia* hope must increasingly have been called into question as time wore on. The deaths of the original generation would certainly have augmented such anxiety and may well

1. Introduction

have produced the soul searching that is recorded here.

2 Peter 3 reflects an obvious embarrassment about the problem of the eschatological delay and the author proposes a solution to it. He addressed the issue, first of all by asserting the reality of judgment in a further reference to the Flood (3.5-6), and secondly by adducing an argument based on Ps. 90.4 (3.8). This text is presented as scriptural proof that the timescale of the *parousia* might be protracted. The Lord was not slow in keeping his promises, the author argues, but he was deliberately biding his time so that no one need perish (3.9). This statement is then combined with the assertion, rooted in the earliest Christian eschatology, that the 'day of the Lord' (itself an important Old Testament phrase) would come 'like a thief' (3.10; cf. Mt. 24.43). This juxtaposition of uncertainty and assurance represents an early attempt to retain the traditional basis of the Christian eschatological hope at a time when its obsolescence was already beginning to be recognized.

The saying about the thief in the night is combined with other elements reminiscent of an apocalyptic eschatology. The author asserts that the heavens would disappear with a roar, the elements be destroyed by fire, and the earth and everything in it 'be found' (3.10; the last phrase is difficult to understand). Warnings about future destruction then lead to the call for moral behaviour: the author says that holy lives were needed in view of the imminent cataclysm (3.11-12). It is repeated that the heavens would be destroyed by fire and that the elements would melt (3.12). The author also anticipates a new heaven and earth, similar it seems to that envisaged by Rev. 21.1 (3.13).

3.15 reasserts the conviction that the Lord's patience meant salvation as 'our beloved brother Paul' is reported as saying. 3.16 says that this theme (evidently that of patience) is found in all the Pauline letters and adds the admission (no doubt to the relief of some modern readers!) that they contained some difficult passages; the author noted that some people distorted Paul's teaching. This is an important reference to the collection of New Testament documents which was being made in the later first century. 2 Peter ends with a warning to readers not to be carried away by lawless people (3.17) and a further exhortation to grow in the grace of 'our Lord and Saviour Jesus Christ', together with a doxology addressed to Jesus (3.18).

The Relationship between Jude and 2 Peter

This Guide takes the view that Jude was written before 2 Peter and that the author of 2 Peter used Jude to frame his response to the false teachers of his own day. The reasons for holding this view must now be considered before we can proceed to examine matters of authorship and dating.

The evidence on which this conclusion is based can be stated briefly. 2 Pet. 2.1-18 and 3.1-3 show clear signs of similarity to Jude 4-13 and 16-18. The contact between the texts is not a precise one: both texts have allusions not found in the other (see Jude 11 and 2 Pet. 2.5; 2.7-8) while roughly the same kind of language is used to combat *different* kinds of false teaching in 2 Peter 2.1-18 and Jude 4-13. The language used is often close but it is by no means always identical, and 2 Peter uses a form of Greek whose style and vocabulary is very different from Jude's.

There are three possible explanations of this evidence. Either both letters were written by the same person; or both used a common source; or one of the two writers used the other document. This third explanation itself has three possible forms: either Jude used 2 Peter, or the other way round, or else one document was conceivably interpolated by the author of the other.

The theory of common authorship claimed a major supporter in John Robinson (1976: 192-95) but it seems an unlikely explanation of the evidence. It ignores the substantial literary and stylistic differences between the texts (for which see e.g. Bauckham 1983: 6, 135) whatever similarities there may also be. This is especially true if the two letters are regarded as close contemporaries. There is a parallel for this situation in the relationship between Colossians and Ephesians, where the Tychicus passage (Col. 4.7-8 = Eph. 6.21-22) is strikingly similar in the two texts but where major differences of style and theology otherwise exist between them. This makes it implausible that the same

1. Introduction

person should have written the two letters. If 2 Peter was written by the same author as Jude we must surely assume that they were written within a relatively short time of each other, given the amount of common material; but this theory fails to explain the differences in thought between the texts, especially the introduction of the material about the *parousia* and judgment in 2 Peter.

The case for a common source is stronger. Its most notable exponent is B. Reicke (1964: 148, 189-90) who thought that both authors used a common sermonic pattern. While many commentators object that, given the extent of the overlap, this source must have been virtually identical with Jude so that it was more likely Jude himself, Bauckham draws attention to the appeal in Jude 20-23 as the most important part of that letter and argues that the author of Jude *might* have been citing such a source in the earlier verses (1983: 141-42). Even he, however, recognizes that this is a complicated hypothesis and that it leaves some ends untied.

For this reason it is best to consider the theory of literary dependence. The work of Neyrey (1980) and Fornberg (1977) is important here. Both scholars applied redaction-critical methods to the two letters and argued that they use similar material to address a *different* situation. These commentators, along with Cranfield (1960), Kelly (1969) and Bauckham (1983), accept that 2 Peter used Jude and not the other way round. It is surely easier to suppose that this was so and that the author of 2 Peter both expanded and edited Jude's biblical allusions for Gentile readers than to explain why Jude should have omitted large parts of 2 Peter, including the reference to a character as familiar as Noah (2 Pet. 2.5), but also have introduced the more obscure references to Cain and Korah (Jude 11) which require knowledge of post-biblical interpretation. Bauckham mentions another argument for the priority of Jude (1983: 142). This is that Jude 4-18 with its catena of biblical allusions has been very carefully composed while the structure of the corresponding passage, 2 Pet. 2.3b-18 (esp. 2.10b-18), seems altogether looser. Those who wish to find support for the opposite position, that Jude used 2 Peter, must turn back to the commentaries of Spitta (1885) and Bigg (1901) to find it. The alternative form of argument, that 2 Peter was interpolated by Jude (mentioned by Guthrie 1990: 816), has failed to command wide assent in scholarship.

Given this conclusion, it is important to reiterate the point that the author of 2 Peter was not just a plagiarizer of Jude but someone who made creative use of the earlier material, notably by its application to a different situation. It cannot be stressed too strongly that 2 Peter was written for a different purpose than Jude. Just because 2 Peter is pseudonymous does not make its life setting fictitious; like Ephesians, 2 Peter is innovative rather than simply imitative. And the fact that 2 Peter makes use of Jude does not mean that the situation addressed was any less specific—simply that it was different.

Who Wrote the Letters?

The likelihood that 2 Peter is pseudonymous makes it impossible now to discover the real author's identity. This is true also for Jude if that letter is judged pseudonymous but the case for doing this is weaker than with 2 Peter. We must now ask what can be learned about the authors of the two documents.

2 Peter claims to have been written by Peter (1.1; 1.12-18; 3.1-2). This attribution is almost universally rejected by commentators. In the first place considerable problems arise from comparing 2 Peter with 1 Peter. 2 Peter displays a great difference in style and vocabulary which Jerome was the first to observe (*Ep.* 120.11). Jerome resolved the difficulty by suggesting that Peter used two scribes, but this conclusion must not be allowed to mask more substantial differences which are thematic and theological rather than simply stylistic. Examples include 2 Peter's attitude to scripture: 1 Peter characteristically cites portions of Scripture (e.g. 2.6) whereas the author of 2 Peter prefers to preserve (with modifications) the catena of scriptural allusions that he inherited from Jude. Eschatology is another area of difference. 1 Peter speaks of 'the revelation of Jesus Christ' (1.7; 1.13) but 2 Peter of his 'coming' (3.4) or of the 'Day of the Lord' (3.10; cf. 3.12); 1 Pet. 1.9 refers to 'the salvation of your

1. *Introduction*

souls' but 2 Pet. 1.11 to 'entry into Christ's eternal kingdom' (see Kelly 1969: 235-37). Moreover 1 Peter has a general application (1.1-2) while 2 Peter seems more obviously designed to meet a specific situation in an unnamed church.

These considerations make it unlikely that the author of 1 Peter was also the author of 2 Peter. On the other hand, it seems likely that the writer of 2 Peter *knew* 1 Peter. This is suggested, both by the fact that 2 Pet. 3.1 refers to an earlier letter of Peter, for which 1 Peter is the only plausible candidate, and by the reference to Noah in 2 Pet. 2.5 which finds an obvious parallel in 1 Pet. 3.20.

The difficulty of seeing 2 Peter as authentically Petrine is compounded by the extent of its dependence on Jude. Would the real Peter not have appealed to his own authority rather than extensively cite a document not by an apostle? Moreover, Peter evidently died in the Neronian Persecution of 64 CE. The time that would have been needed for Jude to become known in Gentile Christian circles makes the hypothesis of genuine Petrine authorship difficult to sustain for 2 Peter even if we accept that Jude is authentic. So, too, the Petrine touches in 2 Peter (e.g. 1.12-18; 3.1-2) seem very contrived and are probably better explained as a later writer's striving for authenticity rather than as Peter's genuine reminiscences. The hypothesis that 2 Peter is pseudonymous is thus a better explanation of the evidence than the suggestion that it is a genuine apostolic writing.

This is certainly not to present the real author as someone who deliberately set out to deceive his readers. They would have known the literary convention and understood the desire for continuity with apostolic authority much better than Western readers today. Nor, of course, does denying Petrine authorship in any way reduce the value of 2 Peter for use today, where it plays an important part in the eschatological debate among other subjects.

The authorship of Jude is more difficult to decide. The letter claims to have been written by Jude, who is called a servant of Jesus Christ and a brother of James (v. 1). There were several Jameses in the early Church. The most famous is the James (called the Just) who was the brother of Jesus. This James became the leader of the Church in Jerusalem after Pentecost as we know from Acts and Galatians (Acts 12.17; 15.15; cf. Gal. 2.2, 12). He, too, is credited with writing a New Testament letter (James) although doubts have been raised about the authenticity of this ascription. The two James' who featured among the disciples of Jesus must also be mentioned. The most famous is James the brother of John and son of Zebedee who was called by Jesus at the start of his ministry (Mk 1.19 and parallels). That this James belonged to an 'inner circle' of disciples is suggested by his presence with Peter and John at the Transfiguration (Mk 9.20) and also probably by his request for future glorification in Mk 10.37. He was put to death by Herod Agrippa in 42 CE (Acts 12.2). Mention must also be made of 'James the Less', the son of Alphaeus, who appears in Mk 3.18 and elsewhere but this James is much more of a 'minor character' in the Gospel story than the son of Zebedee.

The James mentioned at the beginning of Jude is almost without doubt James (the Just) the brother of Jesus. James the son of Alphaeus is really too insignificant to be considered and the death of the son of Zebedee within about ten years of the resurrection makes him too an unlikely candidate. The fact that 'James' is introduced without qualification or further description points inexorably to the figure of James the Just. James in v. 1 is mentioned in the same breath as Jesus. This juxtaposition of names, 'James' and 'Jesus', is naturally explained by the family connection which thrust this James to prominence in the Jerusalem Church ahead of the apostles even though he had played no real part in the ministry of Jesus (see Bauckham 1990b on Jude and the relatives of Jesus). There is evidence from a person called Hegesippus, which is preserved by Eusebius, *Hist. Eccl.* 4.22.4, that James was succeeded in his position by a relative called Symeon so that dynastic considerations were apparently important in the early years of the Jerusalem church (see Bauckham 1990b: 82-94). James was probably a younger brother of Jesus. The theory that he came to faith only after the resurrection, which is indirectly suggested by 1 Cor. 15.7, although it lacks direct evidence, has much to commend it.

There were also a number of Judes in early Christianity.

1. *Introduction*

The most important is Jude (Judas) the brother of Jesus who is mentioned among James and the other brothers of Jesus by Mk 6.3. Hegesippus, reported by Eusebius, *Hist. Eccl.* 3.19.1–3.20.7, records how two of this Jude's grandsons were hauled before the emperor Domitian in the late first century on suspicion of holding dynastic claims but were dismissed when the emperor found that their hopes were set exclusively on an heavenly kingdom. Another Judas is mentioned by Acts 9.11; this verse is probably the source of the statement in the *Acts of Paul* (a second-century CE text) that Judas the Lord's brother befriended Paul in Damascus (see Bauckham 1983: 14). Other Judes who have been suggested include Thomas the Apostle, whom Syrian Christianity apparently knew as Jude (see Bauckham 1990b: 32-36); Judas Barsabbas (who appears in Acts 15.22, 26, 31); and another Jude whom *Apostolic Constitutions* 7.46 calls 'Judas of James' and makes the third bishop of Jerusalem (though that phrase in Greek really means 'Judas *the son* of James').

The balance of probability for the identification of Jude inclines strongly towards the first of the Judes mentioned here—Jude or Judas the brother of Jesus. Only this identification accounts for the fact that Jude is mentioned as 'the brother of James' in a context where James was evidently a well-known figure. That Jude should call himself a 'servant' of Jesus and not 'the brother of Jesus' reflects the writer's modesty and it probably also reflects Jesus' post-resurrection status as a divine being which made it both irreverent and indeed strictly inaccurate for Jude to call himself 'the brother' of someone who had now transcended human relationships. The letter of James similarly avoids the title 'brother' in its introduction (1.1). Jude's introduction of himself as 'the brother of James' would have had undoubted political significance given James's position at the head of the original Christian community.

It is, of course, a different issue as to whether this Jude really wrote the letter. Opinions have varied on this matter and it bears on the problem of dating. Those who deny that Jude wrote it point to the polished nature of the Greek which it is claimed would not have been written by a Galilean of humble birth (though such a person would probably have *spoken* Greek). Moreover Jude 3 (the comment about the faith *once for all* delivered to the saints) is often thought to signify a distance between this author and the apostolic age and to represent a view which Jude himself would not have taken.

This last observation is perhaps not so great an obstacle to genuine authorship as has been held. The author is simply reminding his readers of the changeless nature of the Gospel. The fact that the apostolic age had passed is a deduction from the text and is not made explicit there. Bauckham (1983: 8-11) rightly notes that none of the features normally associated with 'early Catholicism'—the fading of the *parousia* hope, increasing institutionalization of the church and the crystallization of the Christian faith into set forms—is really obvious in Jude. What we find instead is a letter which without much doubt has its roots in primitive Jewish Christian apocalypticism, and this does not offer convincing evidence that the author necessarily worked beyond the apostolic period. It remains perfectly possible that the Jude identified here could have written the letter, but we do not know enough about his life and thought to be *sure* that he did.

When Were the Letters Written?

The view taken here that 2 Peter is dependent on Jude means that the date of Jude must be examined first. This of course depends on whether Jude is regarded as authentic or pseudonymous. If it is authentic the letter may represent one of the earliest letters in the New Testament. Bauckham notes that Jude *possibly* died as late as 90 CE (1983: 14) but we sadly lack any formal record of his death. If Jude wrote the letter himself there are no real grounds for supposing that he did so at a late date, and indeed he could have been a literary contemporary of Paul. Even if it is pseudonymous the letter need not be dated as late as the Fourth Gospel (c. 100 CE). It would hardly have been written when Jude was still alive; but he might have died fairly early on and been selected as patron for that reason. It is impossible to be precise on this issue beyond noting the strongly apocalyptic

1. Introduction

character of the letter and insisting that its date must correspond with what we decide about the likely origin of 2 Peter. If Jude is authentic the letter perhaps belongs to the period roughly 40–70 CE. If pseudonymous it need have been written no later than 70–90 CE, around the same time that Ephesians was composed.

2 Peter could not have been written before Jude if the prevailing theory is correct. 2 Peter was the target of a famous essay by Ernst Käsemann (1964) which argued that here, perhaps more clearly than anywhere in the New Testament, we encounter an 'Early Catholicism': an understanding of the Christian faith that was bound up with notions of Church order and belief which placed it beyond the apostolic age. Käsemann set 2 Peter in the mid-second century CE which made it the latest New Testament document by far, and he saw the letter as an 'apologia' for primitive Christian eschatology and the author's opponents as Gnostics.

The view taken here is that it would have been exceptional for a document that was written so late to have found its way into the New Testament Canon. The theory of pseudonymous authorship suggests perhaps that 2 Peter was written at a time when people could still remember Peter rather than when he was simply a legendary figure. Moreover, Käsemann's theory was bound up with the belief that the author's opponents were Gnostics. Gnosticism was a second-century complex of religions which posited a mythological cosmogony and which taught the hope that the soul might make its way back to the heavenly realm after death. Nothing in 2 Peter conclusively indicates that the opponents were Gnostics. Although Käsemann is right in his assumption that 2 Peter, if the opponents were Gnostics, could not have been written much before the middle of the second century, Neyrey (1980) has proposed the more convincing theory that 2 Peter's opponents were influenced not by Gnosticism at all but by Epicureanism (see also Neyrey 1993: 122-28). Epicureanism was a form of philosophy, much older than Christianity, which was sceptical about divine providence and the issue of retribution after death. Such a background would cogently explain why the opponents addressed by 2 Peter were sceptical about the possibility of the Lord's return and judgment.

If Epicureanism is the background to their belief, 2 Peter could have been written in the late first or early second century CE when Peter was a living memory in the Roman church. The contact between the saying of the 'scoffers' reported in 2 Pet. 3.4 and a similar report in *1 Clement* 23 (96 CE) suggests that 2 Peter was written around this time. Equally, it could not have been written much before about 70 CE to judge from the author's use of Jude. Bauckham sees 3.4 as a response to the immediate crisis provoked by the deaths of the first Christian generation and dates 2 Peter to the period c. 80–90 CE (1983: 157-58). This estimate should perhaps be regarded as a helpful median between conservative and radical assessments.

Why Were the Letters Written?

Both Jude and 2 Peter were written to deal with crises provoked by the appearance of false teachers in Christian churches. The tendency of recent research is to see the situations opposed by the two letters as being different from each other. This is the view followed here.

The situation which prompted Jude is alluded to by vv. 4 and 17-18. It seems that certain people had 'secretly slipped in' to an unnamed church (v. 4) and begun to propagate teaching which had a liberal and perhaps an antinomian basis, not least in matters of sex. Verse 4 confirms that they came from outside. The new arrivals had apparently denied the status of angels as guardians of the Jewish Law (the Torah; vv. 8-9) and thus perhaps the moral element of the Law which a Jewish Christian such as Jude, like his brother James the Just, would have regarded as still binding upon Christians. Verse 11 implies in an allusive way that they were trying to lead others astray in these matters in the author's references to Cain, Balaam and Korah. Verse 19 states that these teachers had caused divisions in the community and that they taught people to follow their natural instincts. The same verse says that in the author's judgment they lacked the Holy Spirit, which in the language

1. Introduction

of first-century Christianity is tantamount to denying their Christian authenticity.

It must be said straight away that this information is so general that it would be unwise to seize on known groups of troublemakers from the first century and to set Jude's opponents within that matrix. A healthy pessimism should be maintained about the possibility of being able to identify Jude's opponents with confidence. Nevertheless it is helpful to make a few observations about them (however speculative these may be). Two areas worth exploring are the teachers' external origin and the libertine basis of their message, both of which are clearly expressed by the text. Their external origin appears from v. 4 where the author says that they had 'wormed their way' (NEB translation) into the church in question. A possible reason why the teachers had come to gain entrance into that church is the theory that they were wandering prophets. The teachers are significantly called 'dreamers' in Jude 8. This phrase has a strong Old Testament background. An important element in that background is the ban against dreamers of dreams (i.e. false prophets) made by Deuteronomy 13. False prophecy was a recurrent feature in early Christianity as we know from the late first-century text called the *Didache* which supplies rules for unmasking false prophets (ch. 11). This part of the *Didache* takes a particular interest in the phenomenon of wandering prophecy. It explains how some prophets wandered from community to community and the author is critical of prophets who stayed too long in one place. Perhaps Jude's opponents were wandering prophets like this, people who claimed inspiration by the Spirit and who travelled from church to church and were held in great respect. In this case their presence in the community would initially have been achieved by legitimate means.

The likely antinomian basis of their teaching also deserves exploration. We can surmise that the teachers were antinomians from hints throughout the letter, especially the references to slandering the angels (vv. 8-9). We do not know whether they had said that the Jewish Law was redundant but they may have done this. That would have seemed shocking to Jewish Christians like Jude and James. Jewish

Christianity also tended to be suspicious of people like Paul who questioned the need for circumcision among Gentile converts. This was seen initially as a denial of the value of the covenant, and it remains an open question as to whether the debate about circumcision was actually settled by the Jerusalem Conference (as Acts 15 says that it was).

The fact that the author criticizes the teachers for 'lacking the Spirit' (v. 19) seems most natural in a situation where they had been boasting of their spiritual prowess. This boast perhaps involved the claim that their life in the Spirit had freed them from the need to live by a written moral code. Their behaviour probably did not set out to be antinomian and it may have involved the expressed intent to 'follow the Spirit' wherever he led. And yet then as now, guidance by the Spirit always involves human interpretation. Two different people, both claiming spiritual inspiration, may come to completely the opposite conclusion about what this involves—especially in a diverse social world which knew the sharply different moral standards of Judaism and paganism. Paul's letters contain the hint that the Jewish covenant was redundant (see Gal. 4.21-31; 2 Cor. 3.7-18). Paul also found problems at Corinth where some Christians thought that it was permissible to eat meat that had been sacrificed to idols (1 Cor. 8) but others disagreed, and where some again boasted that they had greater spiritual gifts than others (1 Cor. 12–14).

Perhaps the teachers had heard the Pauline gospel and argued from the basis of their spiritual freedom in Christ that more liberal forms of behaviour were permissible. They may even have claimed Pauline support for what they said, although Paul's comment that freedom in Christ meant obedience to the 'law of Christ' (Gal. 6.2) suggests that he would not have agreed with them. This is simply a theory about how the teachers might have come to their position and we have no way of substantiating it. Paul, however, was a significant influence in the early Church and the dispute about what kind of behaviour was permissible does seem to have a basis in the wider problem of whether Jewish moral standards (such as are advocated by the author) were still binding. It must be repeated that we know very little about

1. Introduction

the troublemakers, as indeed about the church in question, except what can be deduced from the letter. This makes any interpretation of the situation very tentative.

We can rule out the suggestion that the teachers were 'Gnostics' (for which see e.g. Sidebottom 1967: 69, 79). Gnosticism was a religion which flourished in the second century ce and which promised people liberation from the flesh together with the soul's repatriation with its true heavenly home. Both the likely date and the contents of Jude argue against the thesis that the teachers had a basis of this kind. There is no trace either of cosmic dualism or of other distinctive Gnostic ideas in Jude. It is true that Gnosticism had an antinomian strand but this does make all antionomians in the ancient world Gnostics. Jude's probable origin in the first century casts considerable doubt on the view that the opponents in question were 'Gnostics'.

Turning now to 2 Peter, we are justified in concluding from its author's use of Jude that there were analogies between the situation which he addressed and that addressed by the earlier letter. This should not be allowed to yield the conclusion that the situation was identical, however. 2 Peter includes material that is not found in Jude (notably the defence of the *parousia* hope) and it uses the common elements in a different way. Neyrey (1980, 1993) has offered a valuable insight into the position adopted by 2 Peter's opponents in his demonstration that their eschatological scepticism resembles Epicurean ideas. On this view 2 Peter gives us a rare insight into how people with an interest in Hellenistic philosophy reacted to Christian teaching in the first century CE. They evidently found the eschatological basis of the religion difficult and regarded it as absurd that God would stoop to the lengths of punishment suggested by 2 Pet. 2.4. The teachers presumably also argued that, although God or the gods existed, these did not concern themselves with the human world. The author of 2 Peter wrote to remind his readers of the reality of future judgment, which he did by citing a variety of earlier authorities.

As with Jude's opponents we should beware of the attempt to portray the opponents in 2 Peter as Gnostics for much the same chronological and theological reasons. The teachers may have questioned Christian beliefs about the *parousia* and future judgment but there is no evidence that they reinterpreted these to yield a view of cosmic immortality, still less a cosmogony like that found in Gnostic literature. They seem rather to have been sceptics in the best sense of the word. They were people motivated by a desire to rid Christianity of what were seen as dubious ideas. The author regarded this modernism as a threat because of his convictions about eschatology which stood at the heart of his Christian belief.

Where Were the Letters Written and Addressed?

The questions of where the two letters were written, and to which church or churches they were sent, are difficult and can be answered only indirectly. Jude's interest in Jewish literature, particularly its author's use of *1 Enoch*, suggests that it was written somewhere in Palestine. The addressees are more difficult to discern. Readers are presupposed as having extensive scriptural knowledge, including knowledge of extra-canonical literature, which means perhaps that the church was either predominantly Jewish or else at least contained Jewish people in positions of authority, but it would probably be wrong to say that it was *exclusively* Jewish given the cosmopolitan nature of major cities like Jerusalem and Antioch in the first century ce. Readers apparently also accepted the eschatological tradition of divine intervention and judgment without reservation. This perhaps suggests a readership somewhere in Syria or Palestine, but there is no way that we can be certain about this or speculate more closely on which church is addressed in the letter.

2 Peter by contrast has strong connections with the church in Rome. Commentators have often remarked on its unusual nature both stylistically and theologically when compared with the other New Testament writings. It has affinities with two other documents that are associated with Rome: *1 Clement* and the *Shepherd of Hermas*. There are links with *2 Clement* as well but that text has sometimes been associated with Corinth rather than Rome. Links with *1 Clement*

23 are particularly obvious in 2 Pet. 3.4, the report of the scoffers' eschatological scepticism. There seems no strong possibility that the author of 2 Peter used *1 Clement* or *vice versa*. The connection between the two letters is rather to be explained as the use of common material which circulated in the Roman church in the later first century ce. In support of this projected Roman origin of 2 Peter is the letter's ascription to Peter before his death (1.14), which, tradition has it, took place in Rome. The letter perhaps represents a missive sent by the Roman church, like *1 Clement* (which was addressed to Corinth), to a church or churches for which it felt concern. It was written to reassure readers that what the apostles had said was true (especially about eschatology). It is not possible to ascertain the readers' identity; but since *1 Clement* was sent to Corinth a destination outside Italy may be considered.

The statement of 2 Pet. 3.15-16 that the recipients had also received a letter from Paul has not surprisingly stirred commentators to speculation. Almost all the Pauline letters have been suggested together with the theory of a lost letter. Perhaps the only thing that can be said with confidence about this reference is that it does not permit an unambiguous identification of the recipients. It seems preferable to consider a range of possibilities than to decide on a particular church in the absence of conclusive evidence to support the identification. On the basis of this evidence, however, a destination somewhere in Greece or Asia seems quite likely.

The Two Authors as Interpreters of Earlier Material

One of the most interesting aspects of the letters is the way in which both make use of earlier material: Jude of biblical judgment stories and 2 Peter of Jude's work and the Jewish Testamentary genre. Charles (1993) argues that Jude resembles a 'word of exhortation' discourse. He shows that this had its own distinctive method which involved first the citation of an historical example and then interpretation combined with exhortation. This form is found in both Hellenistic Jewish and early Christian literature. There is a good example of it in Acts 13 where Paul recounts Israelite history, cites and interprets Old Testament material, and draws a conclusion that was designed to show to his audience in Pisidian Antioch the significance of what Jesus had achieved.

We can see the author's use of this method in Jude 5-7. The story of the Exodus from Egypt is followed in the biblical text by that of the destruction of unbelievers (Num. 14). The rebellion of the Watchers in Genesis 6 and the sin of Sodom and Gomorrah are said to have similarly incurred punishment. Jude cites these incidents and calls them an 'example' for people in his own day (v. 7). The term 'example' says much about the author's use of Scripture. He uses the stories to argue that the reality of punishment for sin had been displayed in Israelite history and that what had happened to sinners then would happen again in the experience of the church addressed. On this view sin would always be followed by punishment as the Scriptures had said. The fact that the author speaks in triplets seems intended to prove the fact of judgment beyond doubt on the authority of more than two witnesses (cf. Deut. 19.15). The letter includes a series of such examples to reinforce the severity of its message.

This use of earlier material forms the heart of the writer's literary strategy. Some three quarters of this, among the shortest of the New Testament letters, is given over to typological exhortation which gives the message an unrelenting character. It leaves no doubt that those who followed the teachers would be punished but that the faithful would gain eternal life (v. 21). As Charles says (1993: 167), the author is 'seeking to strengthen the faithful by painting in graphic terms the fate of the unfaithful'. The form of the material does much to convey this message. Although we cannot be sure about the response which the letter produced, its rhetorical effect must have been comparable to that of longer and better known New Testament letters. The message is certainly easier to follow than the argument of Romans. Its starkness is its strength: Jude's literary strategy allowed the biblical images to speak for themselves which they do with conviction through being put together as they are here. We find in Jude a collocation of familiar images which are used in a new way, and it is likely that this reworking of imagery itself helped to create the author's portrait of the teachers and to suggest the response which this was designed to secure.

That 2 Peter's author used Jude says much about the status of Jude and the authority which it was believed to possess in the early church. This author used Jude for the same reason that the author of Jude had used the Old Testament. This was the motive of gaining authority for what was said. The incidents that Jude cites were regarded as authoritative because they were drawn from recognized literature. The use that 2 Peter made of Jude was due to the recognition that 'Jude' was an authority in his own right, doubtless because he was believed to be the brother of James the Just and thus of Jesus himself.

It is fascinating to observe the different ways in which the author of 2 Peter tries to gain authority for his condemnation of the false teachers. He does not appeal to his own status (unless the letter is regarded as authentic). Besides citing Jude he refers to Peter (1.16-18; 3.1), the Old Testament writings (1.19-21) and to Paul (3.15-16). This represents a cumulative attempt to undergird his criticism of the false teachers (2.1) by the citation of different authorities which reveals much about the nature of Christianity when the letter was written. It suggests that a sense of distance from the apostolic generation had already been recognized. This sense of distance explains why pseudepigraphy was a reasonably common feature of the later New Testament literature. So great was the impact made by Jesus, seen in the light of his resurrection and current position as the Lord, that those who had personally known him or had received a special commission from him were granted a unique and irreplaceable status in the church. 2 Peter thus represents an important 'test-case' (and within the New Testament canon) for the exalted status of the original cast of Jesus' followers at a period considerably less than a century after the resurrection.

For Further Reading

Bauckham's commentary (1983) was found indispensable in the preparation of this Guide, while Neyrey (1980) does much to explain the Epicurean basis of the opponents addressed by 2 Peter. His

1993 commentary interestingly applies social scientific methodology to the literature which yields some useful insights. The commentaries of Cranfield (1960) and Kelly (1969) are now perhaps slightly dated but they contain valuable material. Fornberg's study of 2 Peter (1977) also represents an attempt to interpret the letter in its social context. Other literature has been mentioned in the text of this chapter, and there are a number of different classifications in the bibliography for those who want to read further. Chester and Martin (1994) was received only after this manuscript had been completed.

2
READING JUDE

IN THIS AND THE NEXT CHAPTER the two letters will be examined in more detail using the commentary form. Given the prevalent scholarly theory that Jude was written before 2 Peter, Jude will be taken first and its allusions to earlier literature explained.

The Introduction

Jude calls himself a 'servant' of Jesus Christ as well as a brother of James (v. 1). 'Servant' language was familiar in early Christianity and was used in letter-openings by both Paul (Rom. 1.1) and James (1.1). It has a strong Old Testament background where the phrase is predicated of Abraham (Ps. 105.42), Moses (Neh. 9.14) and other major figures. Jesus himself is recorded as using 'servant' language, including the metaphor of giving his life as a 'ransom for many' (Mk 10.45). One of the earliest christological confessions we possess—that in Phil. 2.5-11—says that Jesus adopted a servant's or slave's form (Phil. 2.7), perhaps because crucifixion was the method of execution which the Romans used for slaves.

Jude's self-introduction as a 'servant' of Jesus mirrors both this Old Testament background and the impact of christology where Jesus was. Doubtless there was a strain of rhetorical humility in the fact of senior figures addressing themselves by this title (cf. Paul in Rom. 1.1). Jude significantly refrains from calling himself the 'brother of Jesus' (as does the author of James, 1.1). This reflects both modesty and the belief that Jesus was now the exalted Lord in heaven. There would have been a considerable political importance in the author's calling himself the 'brother of James' given that James the Just was the leader of the mother church at Jerusalem.

Jude has the form of a real letter. Both Doty (1973) and Roetzel (1991: 59-71) have written accounts of the New Testament letter form which repay careful study. Jude deserves to be seen as a letter despite the predominance of its biblical allusions. Charles (1993) has shown that it fits the category of 'word of exhortation' literature in which Old Testament allusions were used to address a contemporary situation. Its author shaped his material with brevity and clarity to leave readers in no doubt about the crisis nature of the situation which confronted them and the choice between judgment and salvation which they must make.

The salutation is anonymous (v. 1b). This is a problem for modern readers but clearly not for the original recipients. These people are said to have been called, loved in God and kept for Jesus Christ. The notion of calling or election again has strong Old Testament precedents (see e.g. Isa. 41.9) and it was a standard theme in Christian literature (e.g. Rom. 1.6-7) and indeed at Qumran (CD 4.4). The love of God, in which God took the initiative in confronting people, formed the basis of all early Christian preaching. It was axiomatic for Christian theology that the Father sent the Son. The latter did not act on his own authority (cf. Jn 3.16; 8.28; Mk 12.6). The assertion that the readers were kept 'for Jesus Christ' is the most difficult statement of the triad and it is sometimes translated (as in the NIV) as being kept 'by Jesus Christ'. Technically speaking the dative is of advantage rather than of agent which gives the former meaning the edge. The phrase refers to the future *parousia* which is anticipated also by the closing benediction (v. 24), when Jesus would appear to carry out the judgment. The language implies that God was keeping the readers and that Jesus would gather them when he returned to commence his reign on earth. There is a note of election here which corresponds with v. 24 where God is worshipped for his ability to keep readers from falling. The language has a strong eschatological orientation. It asserts that those who remained faithful, by which is meant those who resisted the false teaching (and in that sense did what the letter-writer said), would be claimed by Jesus as his own when he returned from heaven.

The qualities mentioned by v. 2—mercy, peace and love— are similar to those said to be the fruit of the Spirit by Paul in Gal. 5.22 ('kindness and goodness' in that passage are the same as 'mercy' here). The thought which joins Jude with Paul at this point is that these flowed from the readers' relationship with God, doubtless in this context with the hint that these virtues must persist so that the verse contains a thinly-veiled ethical exhortation (which is indeed the theme of the whole letter).

The Letter does not specify who the readers were. Some inferior manuscripts say that it was addressed 'to the Gentiles' (v. 1) but this does not feature in the majority tradition and represents a later insertion. We should not conclude too easily that Jude was written as a circular letter. The situation addressed is a specific one and the letter too short (it is only slightly longer than Philemon) to be convincingly regarded as an encyclical. While it is inconvenient that the readers should not be named, this is as it is. We can, however, surmise that readers would have known enough about Jewish biblical exegesis to understand the allusions in the Letter. This includes post-biblical literature so that a Jewish background for many (but probably not all) of them seems likely.

The Cause of the Letter

Verse 3 tells us why the letter was written. The author says that, although he had been eager to write about the salvation which he shared with the readers, he had now found a specific occasion to do this in the need to remind them to contend for the faith that had once and for all been entrusted to the saints. Some scholars have thought that he alludes here to *another* letter that he was about to write and that he changed his purpose on receiving news of the problems in the destination church which he addressed through this more pointed response. This theory must not be dismissed, but even if the author wrote in a hurry we cannot ignore the 'polished' nature of his biblical analogies. It would be interesting to know whether these had achieved something akin to their present form before the writing of this text. The material probably does have a history of exegesis behind it but it is difficult now to reconstruct this in detail. If there were such a background the author's skill would have lain especially in selecting and arranging the material to yield the letter's rhetorical effect. In this way Jude probably offers a badly-needed glance into the nature and contents of the early Christian exhortatory tradition (see further Charles, 1993). We can only guess now at how far such material featured in the teaching of early Christian churches but it probably exercised a prominent role there.

The phrase 'the faith once for all delivered to the saints' denotes a body of teaching that was at a certain time made the subject of authoritative transmission. The noun 'faith' has a dual sense in early Christian literature and denotes both the familiar meaning of 'trusting response' (the well-known Pauline usage) but also the content of Christian teaching (= 'body of knowledge'). 'Faith' is used in Jude 3 more in this second sense of a body of teaching communicated to the saints, although doubtless it also includes the sense of trusting response to God. The phrase has sometimes been held to indicate that Jude was written after the other New Testament letters and that it enshrines an 'early Catholicism' where the content of Christian teaching had become fixed through its delivery to (and by) the apostles in an earlier generation. The nature of 'early Catholicism' is an issue which will be addressed later in this Guide but it must be said here that the concept is in many ways an imprecise one. Nothing in Jude indicates that 'the faith delivered to the saints' in this reference designates a *fixed* body of knowledge. It might well be translated as 'Christian position' or 'Christian truth' and in this context it has more evident ethical implications than doctrinal ones. Jude is not so much countering false teaching about God and about Jesus as censuring the arrogant behaviour of people who thought that they could do whatever they liked. 'Contending for the faith' amounts to a call to virtuous living. The strong sense that this Christian position had been communicated to and by the apostles by no means necessarily sets Jude outside the apostolic period.

The letter is direct and to the point. The introduction and salutation are kept to a bare minimum (as Paul does in Galatians, which was also addressed to a crisis situation). The false teachers are mentioned for the first time in v. 4. The phrase 'certain people' has a pejorative ring (cf. Gal. 2.4, 12). The fact that they had 'slipped in' indicates that they came from outside the community but suggests that they had been able to gain an easy access to it. Their teaching evidently had an antinomian aspect and involved what is called here 'immorality'. This term has a sexual ring. The author rebuffed the teachers by saying that they had used the experience of grace as an excuse for such practices and that their behaviour rendered them 'ungodly'. A similar reserve towards antinomianism is expressed by Paul who said that 'walking by the Spirit' meant not gratifying the desires of the flesh (see Gal. 5.16). Jude states that 'grace' did not mean 'licence' but continued respect for Jesus, who was in all Christian theology the agent through whom grace had been provided.

This criticism supplies the meaning of the comment about 'denying Jesus our Master and Lord' in v. 4. Jude implies that those who behaved immorally (like the teachers) showed that their behaviour had a fundamentally un-Christian basis because it no longer respected the continual lordship of Jesus. 'Grace' as used here has a moral dimension besides its theological implications. The teachers' sense of freedom from restrictions is understood as a denial of grace because it rejected the moral position, which was related to observance of the Jewish Law and especially of its ethical aspect, which Jude deemed important. Their behaviour by implication rendered divine grace inoperative in their lives. The middle part of v. 4 anticipates the scriptural allusions found in the rest of the letter when it says that their condemnation had been 'designated long ago'.

The Scriptural Refutation

Verse 5 introduces the author's scriptural refutation of what the teachers were saying. While this probably carries a predestinarian sense, it also represents a typological form of exegesis. The author asserts that what had happened to people in the past served as a warning to contemporary sinners.

Verses 5-19 are essentially a midrash on earlier literature which collects examples of sin and punishment. 'Midrash' means a creative use of earlier material that places a contemporary interpretation on it. Jude adduces a catena of scriptural allusions to show that the teachers' behaviour had been condemned long ago. Eight different incidents or passages are mentioned (vv. 5-16). These are followed by some words of the apostles (vv. 17-19) which are designed to show that Christian authorities had predicted the teachers' appearance too.

First of all there is the Exodus reference in v. 5. The author says that God had delivered his people from Egypt but that he had then destroyed those who did not believe. The Exodus stood at the heart of all Jewish theology (cf. Deut. 26.8) and it became a familiar metaphor for salvation in early Christianity (see 1 Cor. 10.7-11; Heb. 3–4; Lk. 9.31). This verse alludes to the incident described in Numbers 14 and 26 where the people complained against God on the return of the spies from Canaan and all but Joshua and Caleb were killed as a punishment. The author understood what had happened on that occasion as a type or example of the punishment which would befall the false teachers of his own day and their followers. Like the Old Testament writers he fails to comment on the moral capacities of a God who could act in this way (but this is an important question for interpreters today). The language has a strong rhetorical effect and admonition is its principal function. For those who accepted Moses as authoritative it would leave little doubt about the seriousness of divine retribution and the impossibility of escape from this. The author assumes that the citation of this incident from the Torah, in company with the others mentioned, was a sufficient argument to convince his readers of the peril of their situation.

The one who brought Israel out of Egypt is called 'the Lord'. There is a textual problem here: some important manuscripts have 'Jesus', and one papyrus 'Christ the God'.

2. Reading Jude

It has been disputed in the commentaries whether the term 'Lord' refers to God or to the pre-existent Christ. It is probably best to suppose that author wrote 'Lord' which was then corrected to 'Jesus' and to 'Christ' by the manuscript tradition. It is likely that Jude thought of 'the Lord' in this context as 'God' but it is easy to understand why the early scribes thought that he should have written 'Jesus'. Primitive Christianity universally thought of Jesus as the heavenly Lord who would come for judgment (see e.g. 1 Thess. 3.13). Writers such as Paul in 1 Cor. 10.4 had little hesitation in saying that Christ had been active in Old Testament history (cf. also Jn 8.58; 12.41). It may in fact be pedantic to distinguish between 'God' and 'Jesus' in this reference; Jude, in common with all early Christians, saw Jesus as discharging divine activity (cp. v. 14) so that the two divine beings were closely related in his thought. The ambiguity is thus perhaps a deliberate one. We can at least say that the emphasis falls on the reality of future judgment rather than pedantically on the identity of its agent.

Verse 6 cites the instance of the Fallen Watchers. Gen. 6.1-3 contains the short and enigmatic story of the Watchers who descended from heaven and consorted with human women. The story as told there seems to be an aetiology of human mortality. It describes how the Watchers' sin resulted in the restriction of the human lifespan to 120 years after previous longevity. This is followed in the Genesis story by the description of the Flood which is linked to that of the Watchers (Gen. 6.1-3) and the Nephilim or Giants (Gen. 6.4) somewhat tenuously by the statement that human wickedness had become great (Gen. 6.5) which had made punishment inevitable. Later exegetes were fascinated by this passage, no doubt because of its apocalyptic ambience and its uncertain connection of thought. Some of the earliest post-biblical literature we possess (*1 En.* 6–19) constitutes an elaboration of the story. The Enochic author explains that the Watchers had disclosed secrets to humans (chs. 7 and 8) and he contrasts the mysteries disclosed in this way with the superior information that was imparted to Enoch in the course of his heavenly journey (*1 En.* 16.3). Enochic literature probably circulated quite extensively in

Christian circles, as we know from Jude 14.

Jude's allusion to the angels who had left their proper dwelling (v. 6) betrays a knowledge of this story as retold by *1 Enoch* as well as of the original version in Genesis 6. *1 En.* 10.12 describes how the Watchers were bound beneath the rocks of the earth in preparation for their final punishment. This post-biblical passage supplies the reference to chains and imprisonment which is found in Jude 6. The emphasis in both texts falls on the punishment which awaited those who rebelled against God's order. The fact that the noun 'angels' is placed near the beginning of the verse makes the point that even heavenly beings were not exempt from punishment, with the rhetorical implication that humans would be much less so. Jude implies that those who took God's law into their own hands and acted immorally would suffer the consequences of the Watchers, which was judgment at the final assize.

The next example to be mentioned is that of Sodom and Gomorrah (v. 7). The story of these cities, which is told in Genesis 19, was a notorious example of sinfulness and it described how human beings desired sexual relations with angels. This makes for a clever link with v. 6 (the Watchers story) for the Sodomites' behaviour was the complete opposite of the practices described there, where angels had desired sexual relations with humans. The Sodomites' crime is often thought to have been homosexuality (and this does seem the most obvious interpretation of the Genesis passage; see esp. Gen. 19.5) but in fact this is rarely attributed to them in Jewish tradition (Philo is an exception). The majority of exegetes treat it as a sin against hospitality (see e.g. Josephus, *Ant.* 1.194). The force of the Sodom and Gomorrah allusion in Jude 7 is to censure the immorality which the teachers were advocating and to emphasize the inevitability of punishment for those who behaved in this way.

Verse 8 is the author's commentary on these three allusions which shows why they were appropriate for his message. He calls the teachers 'dreamers', a term which seems based on the proscription of false prophets in Deuteronomy 13 and which shows the false nature of what they were saying (despite any claims they may have made to inspiration by the Spirit). As 'dreamers' or false prophets these teachers 'defiled the flesh', 'rejected authority', and even 'slandered the glorious ones' (i.e. angels). The reference to 'polluting bodies' confirms that sexual malpractice was involved but the precise nature of this crime is left unexplained (for a possible reason see Eph. 5.3). They also 'rejected authority'. Divine authority is meant but perhaps there is the hint that the teachers were contraverting the authority of leaders in the church(es) which Jude addressed as well.

Their 'slander of the glorious ones' is a difficult reference to interpret. That the 'glorious ones' are angels can be ascertained from other Jewish literature (cf. *2 En.* 22.7). A variety of interpretations has been proposed to explain this phrase (see Bauckham 1983: 57-59) but the one which seems most likely is a view of the angels as guardians of the law and of the created order. This view of the angels was common in early Christianity, as we know from Gal. 3.19 and Heb. 2.2, and behaviour which went against the Torah might easily have been construed as slander of its guardians. Paul used an argument based on offending the angels in a different context in 1 Cor. 11.10. On this interpretation the teachers' slander of the angels must have lain in their refusal to accept moral standards, undoubtedly those enshrined in the Jewish Law, which they contravened (and encouraged others to contravene) through their belief that licence was permissible.

This reference to slander is further developed by the story about Michael who disputed with the devil for the body of Moses in v. 9. Most scholars agree that the author draws here on a work called the *Testament of Moses* whose ending, which described Moses' death, has failed to survive. Fortunately there is sufficient information about it in other writers to reconstruct the lost material. Bauckham does so in his commentary (1983: 65-76). He shows that it described how, after Moses' death, God sent Michael to remove his body for burial. The devil opposed this and denied that Moses could receive a decent burial because he had killed the Egyptian in the way recorded by Exod. 2.12. The devil then brought a charge of murder against Moses but this was simply slander and Michael rebuffed him by saying, 'The Lord rebuke you!' The devil then departed and Michael buried the body in the secret place described by Deut. 34.6.

This story makes the point that not even Michael, when he acted as advocate for Moses, felt able to curse the devil on his own authority but recognized God's sole prerogative in doing so. This wider background sets the slander reference in Jude 8 in perspective. Michael's humility is mentioned because it contrasted so obviously with the teachers' arrogance. Their behaviour and message implied that the angels and the Law which they guarded were of small account. The story of the behaviour of the angel chief, who respected higher authority, showed that this attitude was wrong. The author evidently hints that the teachers, as people who claimed to possess religious insight, were astonishingly willing to go against the principles that God had ordained. If Michael had refused to curse even a wicked angel, then much more should they refrain from slighting the duly-appointed guardians of the Law in their teaching and in their behaviour.

This polemical vein is continued in v. 10 which caricatures the teachers' ignorance. They are said to be people who reviled what did not understand. This again seems to be a reference to the importance of the Law on the grounds that it was mediated and guarded by the angels. Moreover, the teachers are said to be behaving like brute beasts and acting 'by instinct as irrational animals do'. This compares their sexual promiscuity with the same unself-conscious passion displayed by animals mating in a field—a far cry from the sophistication to which they aspired. For this reason they would experience destruction (v. 10c), no doubt again at the final judgment which was mentioned by v. 6.

Further Allusions to Jewish Literature

The introduction to v. 11 ('Woe to them...') reminds us of a particular form of oracle, the woe or lament found in the Old Testament prophets (e.g. Amos 6.1). This form was echoed in the preaching of Jesus (Mt. 11.21) and it was used in Palestinian Jewish Christianity (see esp. Mt. 23). Here it introduces another triplet of references to biblical sinners which further censures the teachers' activity. They are said to have walked in the way of Cain, abandoned themselves for profit to Balaam's error, and to have perished in Korah's rebellion.

Cain was notorious in Jewish tradition for being the first murderer (Gen. 4.8). Post-biblical Judaism developed this portrait by making him one who taught others to sin (see Josephus, *Ant.* 1.52-66). The Targums further present Cain as the original heretic and, at least in one branch of the tradition, say that he denied the likelihood of future retribution by God (see Bauckham 1983: 80). Cain thus served as a type of the teachers by enticing others to sin. The analogy perhaps also suggests that they taught that punishment for sin was a fable.

The Balaam reference also draws on Jewish biblical interpretation. Numbers 22–24 tells the story of how Balaam refused to curse Israel for financial reward when asked to do so by Balak. Both Philo (*Vit. Mos.* 1.266-68) and the Targums, however, regard him as having accepted Balak's request in a way that rewrites the biblical story (see also Pseudo-Philo, *Bib. Ant.* 18.13). Like Cain, Balaam was regarded as enticing Israel to sin and hence as responsible for the deaths of the Israelites recorded in Numbers 25. Applied to Jude's situation this example illustrates how the opponents tried to entice others into their loose ways and it also hints that they took payment for doing this.

The Korah reference in v. 11 draws on Numbers 16 where this man and others are said to have led a rebellion against Moses and Aaron. Pseudo-Philo (*Bib. Ant.* 16.1) and one of the Targums (ps-Jonathan to Num. 16.1-2) interpret his rebellion with reference to the passage about the fringes in Num. 15.37-41 about which they complained and subsequently contravened (by making them completely blue; see Bauckham 1983: 83). G. Vermes observes that in later rabbinic tradition Korah claimed that 'the Torah was not from heaven' and accepted only the Decalogue (1975: 173). Korah and his associates thus became almost the archetypal schismatics in Jewish tradition. The author of Jude intended this analogy to censure the teachers' opposition to the Law. He presents those who disobeyed what God had ordained as

Korah's true successors, perhaps again with the hint that they were defying particular (but unspecified) church leaders as much as God.

Jude continues in v. 12 by saying that these teachers were 'rocks' at the Christian love feasts (*agapes*) and that they caroused and fed only themselves. This verse confirms that the teachers were entitled to share the common meal but there is the hint (which follows the reference to Balaam) that they were no more than spongers. The Greek noun *spilades*, translated here as 'rocks', is sometimes translated as 'blemishes' (as in the RSV and by many commentators). 'Rocks', however, is its normal meaning and this makes excellent sense in the context. The teachers were more dangerous than blemishes and they could do considerable damage. As dangerous rocks, the author implies, they were poised to make shipwreck of other peoples' faith.

An important area of danger was in their attitude to the *agape*. The *agape* was the early Christian fellowship meal. We have early evidence for it in 1 Cor. 11.17-22 (which this passage resembles in its hint that the teachers displayed immoderate behaviour at the *agape*, as some had done in Corinth). The *agape* was not simply a Eucharist but included an ordinary meal beforehand. This was combined with the Eucharist until well into the second century. The *agape* was essentially a fellowship occasion in which people of all social classes might participate, and it was a major element in church life at the time. The background to this gathering was the fellowship meals shared by a number of Jewish groups including the Pharisees, and this was a model which Jesus and his disciples had adopted (as at the Last Supper). The teachers evidently treated what was intended to recall the passion of Jesus as no more than a drinking-party, hence the comment here about 'carousing'.

The teachers' self-centred attitude is criticized further in the author's comment that they were 'shepherds who fed only themselves'. 'Shepherds' implies that they had a position of authority in the community (cf. Ezek. 34 from which the image was derived) but the author makes it clear that they were not acting responsibly. Far from thinking about the well-being of those present, they simply satisfied their own needs, so that what should have been an occasion of community rejoicing and solidarity became instead an excuse for self-indulgence. This adds to the charge of sexual malpractice the suggestion that other forms of exuberance were involved as well.

The teachers' insubstantial basis, as people who promised much but delivered little, is further criticized by the second half of v. 12 and in v. 13. They are said to be clouds who promised plenty of rain but were blown away by the wind (cf. Prov. 25.14); trees who bore no fruit (perhaps an allusion to the words of Jesus in Mt. 7.7-17); wild waves of the sea (apparently a reference to the comparison between the sea and the wicked in Isa. 57.20); and wandering stars. This last phrase is another allusion to Enochic literature; *1 En.* 18.13-16 presents the Watchers under the image of stars who transgressed the divine command (cf. also *1 En.* 86.1-6). Like the Watchers, whose fate this allusion recalls, they would suffer the 'nether gloom of darkness' for ever.

Verse 14 incorporates a citation of *1 En.* 1.9. Jude regarded its author as inspired and cited his words by using the verb 'prophesied'. *1 En.* 1.9 is an eschatological prophecy which anticipates God's appearance on earth with the angels to carry out judgment. The author of Jude takes it as a prophecy that 'the Lord', by which he means the Lord Jesus, would appear for judgment so that what was originally a prediction of the theophany is made to anticipate the *parousia* of Jesus (cf. the use of Zech. 14.5 in 1 Thess. 3.13 and 2 Thess. 1.7). Jude states that the reference to judgment described the false teachers of his own day. The idea of impending retribution for sinners, associated with the return of Jesus, determines the way in which this and all the biblical material is used in Jude.

Jude 16 constitutes a further assault on the teachers. The author calls them 'grumblers' and 'malcontents'—another Wilderness analogy (cf. Num. 14.2; Ps. 95.8). They 'grumbled' against the moral laws which God had imposed. This led them to 'follow their own passions', which was the natural result of dissaffection with what God had provided. They were consequently 'loudmouthed boasters'. No Jewish reader of this phrase could fail to remember that the charge of boasting had been laid against the tyrant Antiochus Epiphanes IV by the author of Dan. 11.36 (cf. the similar language in *1 En.* 5.4; 101.3), and as used here it implies that the teachers were boasting against God and thereby demonstrating their own folly. They are also said to have 'flattered people to gain advantage'. This implicitly acknowledges the hold which their teaching had come to exercise but it implies that they may have gained financial advantage from what they were doing (cf. v. 8). Some commentators compare the phrase with *T. Mos.* 5.5 where teachers of Law are said to have perverted justice by taking bribes.

The Words of the Apostles

Verses 17-23 represent the heart of the letter. This passage is central to the argument and not simply an appended ethical exhortation. The author moves from scriptural examples to some words of the apostles whom he says had also anticipated the appearance of false teachers. The source for the saying is not clear (2 Pet. 3.3 is dependent on Jude). What the author says about the ills of the last days resembles passages such as 2 Tim. 3.1-5 and *Asc. Isa.* 3.21-31 but it does not hold a significant amount of language in common with them. It has been disputed whether 'the apostles' mentioned here are the apostolic college in the narrow sense or 'apostles' more widely as emissaries of particular churches. This issue is difficult to resolve since the source for the saying cannot be identified. Both groups may in fact be intended, the one reporting the words of the other.

The reference to the apostles has sometimes led to the suggestion that Jude was written only after the apostles had died (cf. Jude 3). This is not necessarily so. Jude 17 says merely that the apostles had foretold the rise of schisms in the Church as they quite conceivably did (cf. Acts 20.29-30). Writers who believed that the apostles had died generally said so (cf. 2 Pet. 3.4; *Asc. Isa.* 3.21; 4.13). Jude does not, and it is perilous to assume a post-apostolic origin for the letter on the basis of his silence in this matter.

The apostles are reported as saying that 'scoffers' would arise in the final age. 'Scoffers' are defined as people who followed their ungodly desires. 'Scoffers' in the Old Testament (e.g. Ps. 35.16; Prov. 9.7-8; 15.6) were enemies of true religion, moral and religious renegades. The author places great emphasis on the fact that the apostles had predicted their coming. The passage represents an important rhetorical device which is designed to reduce the basis of the teachers' authority. This was done by uniting the testimony of the apostles with that of the prophets to make a concerted point.

The author says further in v. 19 that these scoffers had divided the community, that they were earthly minded people (*psychikoi*), and that they lacked the Spirit. Division was a familiar feature of early Christian churches (see Acts 6.1ff.; and cf. the three Johannine letters). The primitive church simply followed the path of human politics in this; it was by no means a perfect society. Jude, however, is not criticizing 'party-spirit' of the kind mentioned by 1 Cor. 3.3-4 but divisions in the church that had been created by different kinds of *teaching*, which in this case was ethical rather than doctrinal in content. The verse again acknowledges that the teachers had gained a hold in the community but we do not know how the divisions manifested and sustained themselves there. The issue must, however, have been sufficiently serious to have come to Jude's attention and prompted the writing of the letter.

The author says that the teachers followed their natural instincts (v. 19), which is similar in tone to the brute beast analogy of v. 10. This is augmented by the comment that they 'lacked the Spirit' at the end of the verse. That was a damning charge in the context of first-century Christianity where spirit-possession was a universal phenomenon. 'Psychic' and 'spiritual' are used as mutual opposites in Paul's description of the resurrection in 1 Cor. 15.44. Calling the teachers *psychikoi* as opposed to *pneumatikoi* here in Jude implies that they were only aware of the lower aspects of human nature. The statement that they lacked the Spirit effectively meant that they were not true Christians (cf. Rom. 8.9). This comment would have had a particular meaning if the teachers had claimed special expertise in spiritual matters, which is here denied to them. The author by contrast presents obedience to the apostles and to their representatives (no doubt including himself) as the true sign of spiritual progress.

The Call for Perseverance

Verses 20-23 are an exhortatory section which summarizes the message of the letter and which gives clear instructions about how the readers were to behave. They were asked to build themselves up in the faith, to pray in the Holy Spirit (unlike what the author thought that the teachers were doing), and to keep themselves in God's love as they waited for the mercy of Jesus to yield eternal life. The call for 'building up' has a corporate dimension and was intended to counteract the situation of division which existed in the community according to v. 19. The notion of the Church as a building pervades early Christian literature (see e.g. 1 Cor. 3.10-17); Jude does not mention the equally familiar body image (Rom. 12; 1 Cor. 12) but doubtless he knew it. The comment about 'praying in the Spirit' alludes to the universal Christian experience of charismatic worship which included, but which was not exhausted by, *glossolalia*, the habit of speaking in tongues. The phrase again makes for a rhetorical contrast with the teachers who claimed to be men of the Spirit but whom Jude presents as actually lacking the Spirit (v. 19). 'Praying in the Spirit' has an implicit ethical dimension in which genuinely Spirit-filled prayer passed over into appropriate forms of behaviour as a sign of its authenticity.

Readers were further reminded to keep themselves in God's love (v. 21). This interesting phrase again raises the issue of authority as the author saw it. God's love demanded a response from people which it is implied that only those who accepted the author's own position were actually making (or indeed could make). This phrase, like the earlier polemic, conveys the impression that the teachers had moved themselves outside the sphere of God's love, just as they had effectively denied the possibility of grace (v. 4). The result of this, in the terms expressed in the letter, was that judgment would follow. The terminology used here is similar in some

2. *Reading Jude*

respects to the relationship between love for God and membership of the Christian community which features in the Johannine literature and which has an important 'exclusivist' function that lays down the criteria of who belonged to the community and who did not.

As opposed to the teachers and their followers, those who acted on the author's message could expect the 'mercy' of Jesus that would result in eternal life (v. 21b). This was the eschatological benefit of remaining within the love of God. A link between ethics and eschatology, with strongly dualistic implications, is prominent in this part of the letter.

The text of vv. 22-23 is in a state of considerable disrepair and it seems unlikely that it can ever be restored with satisfaction. There are two possible ways of taking the material: that it mentions two categories of people who would receive compassion (the position taken by the NEB) or that it mentions three such categories (the version followed by the RSV). The textual issues are complex and those who wish to find a full account of them must consult the relevant commentaries. We can perhaps take comfort from learning that this is probably the most corrupt passage in all the New Testament writings.

The general meaning can be discerned, however, for all the textual intricacies. The author is calling for compassion towards those who were tempted to follow the teachers, mixed with fear at the fate which awaited renegades. Bauckham (1983) opts for the shorter text as does Kelly (1969) before him. It seems possible that the longer text was expanded from the shorter original (see Birdsall 1963; Osburn 1972).

According to the shorter text those who disputed (some translations have 'doubted') must be snatched from the fire. Others were to be treated with mercy mixed with fear, doubtless in anticipation of the fate which awaited them at the *parousia*. It is not certain whether the author saw the teachers as capable of salvation. He certainly enjoins a rigorist attitude in stating that the community must hate even the clothing that they had touched (v. 23; cf. Zech. 3.3-4). On the other hand it is possible that the teachers featured among those who could be 'snatched from the fire' (v. 23a; cf.

Zech. 3.2). This passage displays a fascinating blend of pity, hatred and superstition about future judgment which does much to expose the mind-set of this early Christian author as he reacted to the threat of false teaching. The letter does not suggest that he had abandoned hope for the community addressed, but it does indicate that he had found it necessary to deliver a timely warning about the consequences of not resisting the troublemakers.

The Doxology

Jude's concluding doxology (vv. 24-25) is the best known part of the letter. It is addressed to God through Jesus, which anticipates the mode of prayer *to* God *through* Christ which Christian theology would later hold correct. The hope that God would keep believers from stumbling has a history in Jewish religious discourse (see e.g. Ps. 38.16) but it receives a specific application here in respect of Christian eschatology. The passage looks forward to the time when God would bring believers *through Jesus* blameless into his presence, for which he was given universal and eternal worship. The converse, implied earlier in the letter, is that those who had failed to mend their ways would perish like the notorious sinners before them.

The Effect of Reading Jude

One of the great uncertainties of reading a letter like Jude (as indeed many early Christian letters) is that we can only estimate the readers' response to it, and we do not know what happened among them after the letter was received. Nevertheless, it is possible to imagine a number of likely outcomes for the situation as it appears from the letter, and such speculation has its part to play in the interpretation of Jude.

The outcome which the author would have preferred is for the teachers to be ejected or at the very least for them to be suppressed. But the teachers may have gained the upper hand, in which case the church addressed would have experienced some kind of division or change. Such change could have had a number of aspects. It might have involved rejecting the *Jewish* Christian position and the turning instead to a Gentile form of Christianity where Paul's teaching was especially valued. Divisions within the community may have resulted in secession or expulsion, hence the formation of diverse groups with different ethical views. It is not possible to decide between these possibilities in the present state of evidence, except of course to say that the author's desired outcome must not be confused with the actual outcome, which remains hidden to us.

It is important also to resist the suggestion that Jude was written only for a *group* within a community, and thus for those who were already disinclined to accept what the teachers were saying. The letter seems designed to exercise a rhetorical appeal to the teachers as much as to those whom the author regarded with greater favour. The author reminded them of the error of their ways and showed that they conformed to the types of biblical sinners. Waverers, or people tempted to side with the teachers, would also have been confronted by this message. As a letter, Jude was probably designed to be read aloud rather than passed from person to person (cf. Rev. 1.3). A natural setting for this public reading would have been the communal *agape*, which gives an added significance to the material in v. 12. It seems likely that the teachers were confronted by the author's rebuke on the very occasion that they chose to indulge some of their favourite vices—as the author no doubt intended that they should be.

We cannot be sure about what effect the letter might have exercised on the teachers. The author must have hoped that they would feel publicly rebuked and so become penitent. One can perhaps imagine their response if this were not the case. The teachers would presumably have caricatured the author as an interfering busybody, someone who was shackled to outmoded ideas and restricted by Judaism, while they themselves were convinced by their relation with the Spirit that more liberal behaviour was acceptable. This response may have included a sharp distinction between the old and the new covenants in which the basis of Jude's appeal to Jewish tradition was used against him as an example of a religious position that had been superseded in Christ. Sadly, we lack the evidence to do anything but state the possibilities. The situation addressed, however, seems to have been a delicately balanced one.

Summary and Conclusion

Jude has often been neglected among the New Testament writings but this is not a true reflection of its importance. The letter has much of the immediacy of Galatians, and for those who know their Bible it is easier to follow than that text. The message is firm and unrelenting: the author says that those who followed the false teachers would perish but that those who resisted them would be saved. The hope for eschatological consummation undergirds the letter as it does most of the New Testament writings. Jude calls for a form of Christianity in which right living played as important a part as correct belief (cf. Jas. 2.24) and where claims to spiritual experience must be tested against the lifestyles of those who made them. Jude repays careful study by those wishing to discover what early Palestinian Christianity was like. Like James it reveals an early expression of Christianity, the Jewish Christian variety, which has now almost vanished from our gaze.

For Further Reading

The commentaries of Bauckham (1983) and Neyrey (1993) are both important, though the former is more detailed than the latter. One of the results of the neglect which Jude has suffered is the fact that there is not nearly so much literature available on this text as, say, on the Pauline letters. The book by Charles (1993) is a notable exception and offers an analysis of the author's literary strategy. Bauckham's book on the relatives of Jesus (1990b) is helpful as well. The need for readers of the Guide to consult the available commentaries must be underscored given the difficult nature of Jude's scriptural allusions.

3
READING 2 PETER

2 PETER, for all its use of Jude, was addressed to a different situation. The author of 2 Peter knew and used Jude as he did other literature. But where Jude was addressed to a readership familiar with the conventions and biblical allusions of Palestinian Jewish Christianity, 2 Peter omits some of its more obscure allusions and introduces another literary genre, that of the Testament. 2 Peter is almost certainly pseudonymous. Peter himself would have been more at home with the thought-world of Jude than with that of 2 Peter, given the latter's polished (indeed at times somewhat overpolished) Greek. Moreover, the information attributing the letter to Peter, like the Pauline touches in Ephesians, seems a little too contrived to be convincing. 2 Peter was probably written by an imitator of Peter a generation or so after the apostle's death in 64 CE.

The Introduction

2 Peter opens with the author's introduction of himself as a 'servant' of Jesus Christ and the added comment that he was an apostle. The apostles were the foundation pillars of the church according to 1 Cor. 12.28 (cf. also the later Eph. 2.20). Paul's letter to the Galatians helps to explain what the term 'apostle' meant in early Christianity. Paul specifically claims to be an apostle in Gal. 2.8 in a context where he is obliged to defend his distance from the Jerusalem hierarchy, and doubtless the criticism made by Judaizing opponents that he had not been part of things from the beginning. His elaborate

defence of his calling and gospel (Gal. 1.15-17), together with his insistence on having seen Jesus (1 Cor. 15.7), suggests that visionary experience of the risen Christ and the sense of commission by him were regarded by Paul as qualifying him for office. This sense of commission by Jesus was thus of the essence of apostolicity, as is suggested also by Mt. 28.18-20.

There had never been any doubt in the Church about Peter's apostolic credentials (unlike Paul's). Peter was one of the first followers of Jesus (Mk 1.16) and he enjoyed a place of special prominence in Gospel tradition as the person who had identified Jesus as Messiah at Caesarea Philippi (Mk 8.29). Matthew adds the comment that this event (probably Peter's confession of faith rather than Peter the person) was the foundation-stone of the Christian church (Mt. 16.18). Although James became the leader of the church in Jerusalem, evidently for dynastic reasons, Peter was closely involved in spreading the Gospel beyond Jerusalem (see Acts 10; Gal. 2.11-14). Tradition has it that he became the first bishop of the Roman church and that he died a martyr in Rome (see Cullmann 1962: 70-153; Thiede 1976: 171-94). 2 Peter is thus attributed to a recognized and important figure in early Christianity, someone who had accompanied Jesus from the beginning and who belonged to the 'inner circle' of his disciples (which comprised Peter, James and John). His choice as patron for this letter was due both to his apostolic credentials and to his association with the church in Rome.

2 Peter lacks any clear identification of its recipients but we need not conclude from this that it is a 'general epistle' (as 1 Peter seems to be). The reference to false teachers in ch. 2 implies that it was addressed to a specific situation. 1.1 says that the recipients had received a faith of equal standing with the apostles'. This comment recalls the comment of Jude 3 but it has a pseudonymous ring. 1.2 follows the salutation form found in other New Testament letters except that the author mentions the 'knowledge' of God as prominent in creating grace and peace. This has sometimes led to the charge that 2 Peter reflects a 'Gnostic' background' but the letter's thought-world is much better explained as a *pre*-Gnostic use of terminology that would

later be employed in a different sense in Gnosticism. 'Faith' here means as much the *content* of what was believed (including the tradition of Christian eschatology) as it does the trusting response of Christians towards God. Knowing God, the author says, brought grace and peace. Both of these are metaphors for salvation which are found elsewhere in the New Testament (e.g. Jn 1.17; Col. 1.20).

Homiletic Instruction

1.3-11 expands the reference to the faith like the apostles' in 1.1. K. Baltzer (1971) shows that these verses follow a homiletic pattern which is found in other Jewish and Christian literature. The homily presented here makes a clear connection between faith and ethics. It is perhaps a little difficult to deduce the reason for the letter from this section. This is because the author writes allusively as if he does not want to describe offensive behaviour directly, but, of course, the original readers knew much more about their situation than we do. 1.3-4 says that God's power had provided readers with everything needed for a godly life and enabled them to 'escape the corruption in the world'. Such corruption is said to have existed 'because of passion'.

The author thus does give at least some clue about the situation when he says that 'corruption' was a significant feature of it. 'Corruption' in this context is a moral term which designates inappropriate behaviour, but it also has eschatological overtones in the hint that corruption brought destruction. This point is reiterated in chs. 2 and 3. It appears from these later passages that the 'corruption' at stake had sexual overtones, which does much to explain the author's use of Jude where a similar situation had been addressed.

2 Peter continues by urging readers to 'become partakers of the divine nature' (1.4). This looks beyond the present life to the prospect of immortality thereafter. Union or affinity with heavenly beings had been part of the resurrection hope in Judaism from Dan. 12.3 onwards. It featured in the teaching of Jesus according to Lk. 20.36, who reportedly denied that the resurrected were restricted by human cate-

gories such as marriage. The author's implication in this passage seems to be that participation in the divine nature began in the present life, where it was forged in the battle with corruption, and that it would finally be complete after death. This view draws extensively on Platonic thought. Hellenistic Judaism had long assimilated the Platonic distinction between form and reality to assert that heaven or the realm of ideas transcended corruptible human experience (see e.g. Plato, *Theatetus* 176ab; and cf. Wis. 2.23). This distinction was developed by Philo of Alexandria in the early Common Era. Philo asserted that union with the divine world was possible through ecstatic experience in this life and that it could be achieved permanently after death (*Quaest. Ex.* 2.29). This literature shows the background to the view expressed here. 2 Peter's hope of 'sharing the divine nature', with its obviously Hellenistic background, came to be a major theme in Christian theology (see Lossky 1957) and it deserves careful consideration in view of what the author says about those who denied the *parousia* in ch. 3.

The author's reluctance to describe vice is matched by his willingness to describe more appropriate behaviour. 1.5-7 introduces a list of virtues which has numerous parallels in Hellenistic literature (cf. also Gal. 5.22). Bauckham (1983: 174-75) observes that the list differs from the majority of New Testament ethical lists both in terminology, since it employs a vocabulary with extensive parallels in Greek popular philosophy, and in form, as the author uses a device called '*sorites*' in which each virtue is repeated to yield a logical progression. To faith must be added virtue, virtue must be augmented by knowledge; the list includes self-control, steadfastness, godliness and brotherly affection. Love comes at the end of the list, as in 1 Corinthians 13 it is made the transcendent virtue.

The order in which these virtues are introduced seems largely random. It is difficult to understand exactly how one was intended to produce the next, and probably wrong to search for precise connections between them. The author intended his list to have a cumulative effect and to demonstrate the kind of lifestyle which he thought a pious Christian should adopt. The *sorites* has the rhetorical purpose of drawing attention to the need to cultivate virtue and it shows the kind of behaviour which proved that 'worldly corruption' was being overcome.

1.10-11 summarizes this link between faith, ethics and eschatology. The writer supports his request that readers should 'confirm their call and election'—doubtless through ethical action—by saying that those who lived such a lifestyle would never fall (1.10b). They would finally enter 'the eternal kingdom of our Lord and Saviour Jesus Christ' (1.11). This last phrase picks up the hope for sharing the divine nature in 1.4 and again anticipates the full reception of eschatological benefits in the afterlife.

Peter's 'Testament'

2 Pet. 1.12 begins a section which is intended to authenticate the claim that Peter was the writer. This in turn substantiates the assertion that what the letter contained was not made-up stories but material gained from vision of the transformed Jesus. The need to find authority is very obvious here. The author uses the device of the Testament to set his own views in the mouth of Peter.

1.12-15 seems much too 'contrived' to have been written by Peter himself. It makes Peter say that he would shortly die (1.14) and that he had committed this material to writing so that it would be remembered after his death (1.15). This passage is followed by the section about the Transfiguration (1.16-18) which is introduced by the assertion that the author did not follow fabricated stories about the 'power and coming of our Lord Jesus Christ' (1.16). Perhaps the opponents had been saying that the doctrine of the *parousia* had been invented out of nothing (see Bauckham 1983: 155). The author responded by describing Peter's vision of the transformed Jesus which he understood to anticipate the Saviour's return from heaven in the *parousia*. The fact that Peter had received an apocalyptic vision of the heavenly Christ is presented as the first strand of evidence that Jesus would return for judgment.

1.19-21 adds a second strand of evidence to confirm the authenticity of Christian preaching about judgment by appealing to the example of the prophets. Old Testament prophets are meant; contemporary Christian prophets are neither mentioned nor obviously intended here. 'Prophets' is probably a term for the whole Old Testament and thus includes all three divisions of the Hebrew Bible (not just the second). The author tells his readers to pay careful attention to these writings. He uses the image of the divine Law as a lamp (which he derived from the Psalter) and said that its witness would last until the day dawned and the morning star arose (1.19). Both of these are metaphors for the *parousia*. The implication is that the Scriptures held authority until the return of Jesus which they had for so long anticipated. The star analogy is an allusion to Num. 24.17 ('A star shall come out of Jacob') which was understood messianically in Judaism as well as is early Christianity.

The exegesis of 1.20 has been disputed. Some scholars think that it refers to the origin of prophecy (and that it means 'the prophet is not speaking his own words') but the majority of commentators refer it to the interpretation of prophecy ('no prophecy is a matter of individual interpretation'). This second view seems the more likely. On this reading of the verse the author insists that nobody can interpret prophecy according to his or her private understanding and states that the meaning of a text must be determined by the Christian community as a whole. 2 Peter thus represents early evidence for an emerging *tradition* of exegesis in early Christianity which was used to counter those who were introducing alternative opinions.

The Teachers and their Fate

The author's literary strategy is to establish the need for ethical action and the authority which undergirds this demand before introducing the situation which had prompted the letter. This situation is introduced in ch. 2. The author says that just as Israel had had false prophets so the recipient church now had false teachers. The name 'prophet' is denied to these teachers as a way of reducing their authority, and this contrasts strongly with what the author said about the value of (true) prophecy in 1.20-21.

This part of 2 Peter makes extensive use of Jude. It represents early evidence for the importance of that epistle in the

3. *Reading 2 Peter* 63

Church and this must not be neglected as evidence that Jude was believed to have come from *the* Jude, the brother of Jesus. Jude's authority is by implication set alongside that of Peter (1.12-18), the prophets (1.19-21) and Paul (3.15-16) so that the author uses a variety of ways of authenticating the message that he presented to the readers.

He says that the teachers had introduced 'destructive heresies' (2.1). The term 'heresy' is a pejorative one and it probably means 'divisions' rather than 'heresy' as we know it today. The 'false teaching' described in the letter is ethical and eschatological but not doctrinal in content. Those who offered it, says 2.1, were effectively denying the Master who had bought them. This metaphor comes from the slave market and its thought is modelled on Jude 4. The teachers' mode of denying Jesus is suggested by the following passage (2.4-10) which polemicizes against sexual immorality. The author says that judgment had long been decreed for them and that it awaited them yet (2.1; 2.3).

Evidence of dependence on Jude, albeit with variations on the received material, is found throughout ch. 2. Bauckham believes that in 2.4-9 the author also draws on a paranaetic tradition that was independent of Jude (1983: 246). The inevitability of judgment for transgression is the major theme of this section. 2.4 is developed from Jude 6. The author says that God did not spare the angels who sinned but imprisoned them in dark dungeons in preparation for judgment. 2.5 mentions the Flood, which is not found in Jude, and explains how God had protected the righteous Noah and seven others. The Flood is mentioned also in 1 Pet. 3.20 and this reference may have been suggested to the author through his use of that letter as well as of the paranaetic tradition (see *3 Macc.* 2.4 and *T. Naph.* 3.5). A reference to the Flood would have been less obscure to Gentile readers than the stories about Cain and Korah which 2 Peter omits.

2.6 cites the case of Sodom and Gomorrah in dependence on Jude 7. The fate of their inhabitants is made an example of what happened to ungodly people. The reference to Lot in 2 Pet. 2.7, which presents him in favourable terms, has no parallel in Jude and was again derived from wider tradition (cf. Wis. 10.6). Lot is said to have been distressed by the filthy lives of those around him (2.7-8). His case is used to explain that the Lord was able to rescue godly people from trials and to hold the unrighteous under punishment until the last day (2.9). The participle 'holding under punishment' is in the present tense and this implies that punishment even now impended over the teachers. In 2.10a the author adds the rejoinder that punishment was especially meted out to those who indulged the flesh and despised authority (as in Jude, perhaps with the hint that the teachers were opposing church leaders approved by the author).

2.10b-11 echoes Jude 8-10. The teachers are now presented as bold and arrogant people who were not afraid to slander celestial beings when angels (who were much more important than they were) did not think to do this. This takes the story in Jude 9, which made the point that God must bring his own rebuke, to indicate angelic respect for other angels, not precisely what Jude had said (see Bauckham 1983: 261). The image as reworked here comments on the arrogance and the ignorance of those who acted in this way.

How the teachers slandered heavenly beings is difficult to understand. Given the background in Jude it seems likely that the beings in question were Satan and his angels and that the teachers falsely believed these had no power over them. More than that we cannot say; but there is a good indication of the hold which angels were believed to influence in Col. 2.15 where Paul says that the power of 'principalities and powers' had been broken (only) by the death of Jesus. The author of 2 Peter probably shared this view of angelic power and marvelled at those who dared to defy it. Their lack of reason made them like dumb animals bred for slaughter, and he said that they would perish in a similar way (2.12).

2.13 further describes the teachers' libertine behaviour. The author says that their idea of pleasure was to 'revel in the daytime'. Unlike the charge laid against the apostles in Acts 2.13, this really does attest the practice of alcoholic excesses among some Christians, made all the worse for the fact that it was done during working hours. The rest of the verse makes two puns on information derived from Jude, which probably indicates that the readers as well as the author knew that text. The author changes *spilades* ('rocks') to *spiloi* ('blemishes') and states that the teachers were 'blots and blemishes' on the Christian body (with the implication that this rendered them unfit for service given the levitical background in Lev. 21.21). He also adapts the reference to Christian love-feasts in Jude 12 and substitutes *apatai* for *agapai* to yield the criticism that the opponents 'revelled *in their deceptions*'. Their revelling was thus not confined to *agapes* but extended to other occasions as well. This reworking of Jude shows the literary self-consciousness which undergirds 2 Peter. In good Hellenistic fashion the author was concerned not just to cite but also to improve his sources. This again is perhaps to be taken as an indication that Peter was not the real author.

2.14 mentions the charge of adultery. The author states that the teachers seduced the unstable and that they were experts in greed. 2.15 introduces the Balaam analogy from Jude 11 (but not the reference to Cain or Korah). Balaam is said to have loved the wages of wickedness, a point that has to be deduced from Jude but which is made explicit here. It also implies that the teachers took money from the church(es) they were troubling. The inclusion of this explanation suggests that the author was writing for a situation where the simple analogy would not have been understood, and thus probably for Gentiles who knew less about Jewish traditions than Jewish Christians. The more obscure Cain and Korah material was omitted for the same reason. Balaam's rebuke by his donkey (2.16) harks back to the description of the teachers as brute beasts in 2.12 and asserts with great irony that the ass showed more insight than they did.

2.17 draws on Jude 12b-13 to emphasize the feckless nature of the teachers and to reiterate their punishment. They are held to be springs without water and mists driven by a storm (this is an expansion of Jude's cloud analogy into two images). Darkness was reserved for them like the wandering stars of Jude 13. 2.18 draws loosely on Jude 16 and explains that the teachers mouthed empty words and enticed people by appealing to lustful desires. The last part of the verse, which states that they enticed 'people who have barely escaped from those who live in error', suggests that recent converts from paganism were especially targeted, perhaps because of their unfamiliarity with the Christian ethical tradition. The notion of arrogant talk is borrowed from Jude 16 where it described slander against God. Here it has a different sense, that of futile talking which may have sounded impressive but which lacked a depth of meaning and which meant that the teachers' 'loud boasts' were simply 'folly'.

In 2.19 the author departs from Jude and describes the teachers in his own words. He says that they promised people freedom but that they themselves were slaves to depravity. The fact that no source is used here makes this perhaps the clearest statement of the teachers' position in the whole letter. Neyrey (1980) argues that this view of 'freedom' involved the rejection of beliefs about future *parousia* and judgment. On his view the teachers thought themselves 'free' from restrictive beliefs and so that they could live as they pleased. 2.20 is a stark description of the position of people who were convinced by such teaching. The author says that, if they had once escaped worldly corruption through knowing Jesus (cf. 1.4) but later re-entangled themselves in it, their final state would be worse than the first (cf. Mt. 12.43-45; Lk. 11.24-26; Hermas, *Sim.* 9.17.5). He adds that it was better never to have heard of righteousness than to turn their backs on the sacred command (2.21; cf. Mt. 18.6). This is followed by two proverbs designed to emphasize the stupidity of what the teachers were doing. Like 2.12, 16, both are based on the animal kingdom: the dog who returned to its vomit (from Prov. 26.11) and the clean sow which wallowed in mud (for which there is a parallel in the Jewish work called the *Story of Ahikar*; 8.18 in the Syriac text). These proverbs, which required no explanation, had the effect of presenting what may have seemed an attractive option (the libertine gospel with its promise of freedom in the Spirit) as folly rather than insight.

The Teachers' Eschatological Scepticism

Chapter 2 thus criticizes the teachers' libertine position and warns readers not to be carried away by what they were saying. This is followed in ch. 3 by a refutation of their eschatological scepticism. In order to understand this section we need to remember Neyrey's point that what they said perhaps had roots in Epicureanism. Epicureans believed that, although the gods existed, they did not concern themselves with the human world so that all talk about divine judgment, including that which the Christians believed would be brought to bear at the *parousia*, were misplaced. Neyrey makes the point that the teachers may have been influenced by Epicurean ideas but that they were not necessarily Epicureans in the formal sense. They rather stood in a wider tradition of scepticism about divine judgment which features in other Jewish literature too.

2 Pet. 3.1 links back to Peter and says that this was now the second letter which the apostle had written to the recipients. This almost certainly reveals knowledge of 1 Peter. 2 Peter, like its predecessor, is said to be a reminder of what had been predicted by 'the prophets' and 'your apostles' (3.1-2). The word order (prophets before apostles) shows that again Old Testament writers and not contemporary prophets are meant (cf. 1 Cor. 12.28; Eph. 2.20, where the apostles precede Christian prophets). The author sees the Old Testament writers as prophets of the *parousia*, as he does in 1.19. The apostles are here called 'your apostles'. This possibly denotes people beyond the apostolic college, specifically those who brought the gospel to the church in question, but it *might* mean those members of the college who had exercised a special responsibility there. What the apostles said was authoritative because it constituted the command which had been transmitted by Jesus ('the Lord and Saviour') through them (3.2). The origin of this material with Jesus himself is stressed at this point (cf. 1.16-18). The words of the apostles had equal status with that of scripture for that reason.

3.3 picks up the thought of Jude 17 to make the point, on apostolic authority, that 'scoffers' would appear in the last days. The letter indicates that 'scoffers' were people who lived self-indulgent lives and who denied the likelihood of a future *parousia* and judgment. Several scholars think that the author followed a Jewish source in this passage, one that was utilized also by the authors of *1 Clem.* 23.3 and *2 Clem.* 11.2 (see Bauckham 1983: 282-85).

These scoffers are reported as saying, '"Where is the promise of his coming? For ever since the fathers fell asleep, all things have continued as they were from the beginning of creation"' (3.4). 'Sleeping' here means death: the verse alludes to the passing of the first Christian generation (cf. *Asc. Isa.* 3.21; 4.13). The death of believers had caused a problem in Pauline Christianity which Paul had addressed in 1 Thess. 4.13-18 and then again in the Corinthian correspondence (1 Cor. 15; 2 Cor. 5). Whereas in the 50s (when Paul wrote) people were disturbed by the deaths of *some* of their friends, nearer the end of the century the demise of many if not most of the original Christians caused the crisis of confidence that is recorded here. While no New Testament document (including 2 Peter, whose evidence on the point is crucial) indicates that *parousia* hopes were abandoned in first century Christianity, 2 Pet. 3.4 (supported by the Clementine literature) is testimony to the fact that some in the church were becoming sceptical about the truth of the promised event. Mk 9.1 records Jesus as saying that some of the disciples would not taste death until they had seen the kingdom's arrival, and this text perhaps had its part to play in creating the belief that the original generation must be alive to witness the coming of the kingdom. The deaths of Peter and others in this case would have prompted reflection about whether the kingdom would come at all.

The 'scoffers' (as they are called here in derogatory terms) thus gave voice to an important issue, perhaps the most important issue, which Christianity had to face in its early years. This was the need to develop the perspective of a Jewish sect dominated by an apocalyptic eschatology into that of a religion which recognized and accommodated itself to the need to occupy a permanent position in the world. This must have been a gradual process and it was hardly complete by the end of the first century. We should not underestimate the role played by 'sceptics' such as these in raising the questions which achieved this transition despite the fact that the author of 2 Peter clearly did not like what they were doing.

3. Reading 2 Peter

The author deals with the problem of eschatological scepticism by appealing again to the example of the Flood (3.5-6; cf. 2.5). He says that the same water which had helped to create the earth later functioned as the agent of its destruction. The image then shifts (somewhat jarringly) to that of fire (3.7). The link with the reference to the Flood is the fact that this form of judgment had also been decreed by God's word. Fire, which had been stored up for the day of judgment, would bring about the destruction of the ungodly (3.7; cf. the Sodom analogy in 2.6). The notion of impending world conflagration is unique here in the New Testament but it became common in later Christian literature (see e.g. Justin, *I Apology* 20.1-2; *Asc. Isa.* 4.18). The idea also featured in Jewish apocalyptic literature although it is by no means universal there (see e.g. *1 En.* 1.6-9; *Sib. Or.* 2.187-213).

The author presents a second argument to counter this eschatological scepticism (3.8-10). He takes an expanded version of Ps. 90.4 ('with the Lord one day is as a thousand years, and a thousand years as one day') to imply that the Lord was not slow in keeping his promise as the scoffers had suggested, but rather that he was patient and desired that everyone should come to repentance. The comment about the Lord not being slow is based on the last phrase of Hab. 2.3, which was an important text for discussing the problem of eschatological delay in Judaism. This use of Ps. 90.4 refers that text to the present order rather than to the future millenarian kingdom, against the sense in which some later writers understood it (see Bietenhard 1953).

The author's willingness to accept the delay (but not the demise) of the *parousia* hope is combined with the apocalyptic assertion that the day of the Lord would come like a thief in the night (3.10a). This alludes to a saying of Jesus which is found frequently in the New Testament (see Mt. 24.43; 1 Thess. 5.2; Rev. 3.3). At the *parousia*, so he says, the heavens would disappear with a roar, the heavenly bodies be destroyed by fire and the earth and what it contained be 'found' (3.10b). The meaning of the phrase 'be found' (3.10) has puzzled commentators. Bauckham (1983: 319) cites with approval an article by W.E. Wilson who suggests that the meaning is that the earth would be found *by God* and thus laid bare to his all-seeing gaze which none could escape. This suggests that a form of primaevalism, which is a feature also of the Pauline eschatology (Rom. 8.18-25), is the crucial issue here (cf. again *Asc. Isa.* 4.18). Several English translations (including the RSV) read the variant 'will be burned' at this point and other commentators prefer the emendation 'will *not* be found'. The phrase was evidently found difficult even in the early manuscript tradition.

The author's eschatological reassurance is used to support an ethical exhortation in 3.11. Like Paul in 1 Thess. 5.6-11 he says that, since everything was destined for destruction, people should lead holy and godly lives. They should look forward to the Day of God when the heavens would be dissolved and the elements melt in the heat (3.12; cf. Isa. 34.4). It is doubtless fair to say that, despite the stern language used, the author's purpose is encouraging rather than threatening at this point. He wanted to advocate perseverance until the end rather than simply to threaten readers with judgment. 3.13 repeats the promise of a new heaven and a new earth from Isa. 65.17 which is found also in Jewish apocalyptic literature (e.g. *Jub.* 1.29; *1 En.* 45.4-5). This promise was an important theme in primitive Christian eschatology to judge from its appearance in writings as diverse as Rom. 8.21 and Rev. 21.1. The author's future hope was thus guided by notions of a perfect (re)creation rather than exclusively by beliefs about judgment. He expected this new order to be 'the home of righteousness' (2.13).

The Conclusion of the Letter

3.14 marks the beginning of the letter's conclusion, which has a mainly exhortatory function. The author says that, in view of what lay ahead, readers should make every effort to be spotless and blameless (cf. 2.13; Eph. 5.27) and be 'at peace with him'. This denotes the eschatological state of being righteous before God with its consequences for the future judgment. The Lord's patience would mean salvation (3.15), an insight that the author claims to find in the Pauline correspondence as well. He mentions a Pauline letter addressed to his own recipients (3.15) as well as an emerging collection of all Paul's letters (3.16). In this 2 Peter represents important evidence for the first moves towards the formation of a New Testament canon.

The problem arises of which Pauline letter is meant here. Almost all have been suggested in the commentaries, together with the theory of a lost letter. It is difficult to resolve this issue. If the church addressed had also been the recipient of 1 Peter (as 2 Pet. 3.1 claims) then Galatians and Colossians seem the most likely candidates given the information in 1 Pet. 1.1 (that it was written to churches in Asia Minor). This is not certain, however, and it is probably better not to speculate too closely than to opt for a particular letter in the absence of decisive evidence.

The author frankly admits that Paul was not easy to understand and says even that people whom he calls 'ignorant and unstable' twisted what Paul had said (3.16). He also says that these people misused other Scriptures as well (4.16b). These further writings are not identified but the author's use of the noun *grafe* (= 'writing') suggests that the Old Testament is meant. Paul's letters are thus given the same authoritative status as the Hebrew Bible for Christian readers within half a century of the apostle's presumed death.

The letter closes by offering a further warning to readers to be on their guard and not to be carried away by the error of lawless people. In contrast readers must try to grow in the grace of their Lord and Saviour Jesus Christ, who is magnified through a short doxology (3.18).

What Effect Does 2 Peter Make on Readers?

2 Peter is a difficult text, not least because of the self-conscious character of its Greek but also because its progress of thought is sometimes hard to follow. Much of the style and diction in the letter is deliberately 'polished'. The pseudepigraphy is also alien to modern readers, as is perhaps the author's deliberate but unacknowledged use of Jude.

Perhaps the most important issue in the letter is the affirmation that divine judgment would take place despite what the teachers had claimed. The eschatological argument is related to the ethical argument inasmuch as the teachers were apparently saying that licentious behaviour was permissible because any notion of divine intervention and punishment was false. The author makes a strong link between correct behaviour and acceptance by God at the *parousia* (see e.g. 3.11) with the implication that those who did wrong would be punished.

The author's answer to the problem posed by the eschatological scepticism seems to have been the old adage that 'time will tell'. Belief in judgment would be seen to be justified only when judgment took place. Readers were encouraged by the fourfold witness of the Old Testament, Peter, Paul and Jude to accept that what Christianity had believed about the *parousia* was true and that the event would take place when God deemed the time appropriate.

As with Jude, we do not know what effect 2 Peter actually produced on the situation which it addressed. The teachers would presumably have dismissed further predictions of judgment with the same scepticism that they had treated existing statements about the *parousia*. This was perhaps done by asserting that God did not concern himself with the world so that notions of future retribution were fictitious. We do not not know enough about the opponents to comment on the extent to which they had assimilated Epicurean ideas, nor do we actually know whether these teachers were full and active members of the church or simply figures in wider society who had influenced church members.

The author's eschatological argument would have appealed more naturally to those who were already inclined to accept it, so that eschatology doubtless remained a fundamental area of difference between the author and his opponents. The uncertainty of the eschatological timescale, although in one sense an embarrassment to the author, is also the means by which he reinforced his appeal to sympathetic readers. He says that it was precisely because the timing of the *parousia* was uncertain that they must be prepared for it at any time (ch. 3). This author also extends his understanding of eschatology to accomodate every eventuality. He allows for the possibility of sharing the divine nature after death as well as for an encounter with the Lord by the living at the *parousia*. This refusal to be specific about when the judgment would take place would doubtless have appealed to people who were still inclined to accept arguments about divine intervention and providence. It mirrors normal human uncertainty about matters of life or death and underscores the offer of salvation with the threat of punishment.

This eschatological uncertainty, which may have been welcomed by some of the original readers, has become an undoubted obstacle in the interpretation of 2 Peter today. 2 Pet. 3.3-13 more than any other passage in the New Testament has led to the belief that Christianity can continue to expect the return of Jesus even though the event continues to be delayed. There seem to be reasons for questioning this view. Although the author accepted that the timescale might be protracted, it seems doubtful whether he anticipated that the delay would be as extensive as it has actually proved to be. *All* of those readers who were told to expect the Lord like a thief in the night are now dead, as are countless later Christians. Many Christian theologians today would regard it as hazardous to give the *parousia* a central position in their doctrinal reflection given the failure of early Christian eschatological hopes and what seems now to be effectively the permanent delay of the event. The idea of 'sharing the divine nature after death' (however this is interpreted) seems a much more relevant idea for the construction of a contemporary Christian eschatology.

This comment must not be allowed to mask the fact that 2 Peter shows New Testament (and indeed Christian) eschatology at an important stage of transition. The uncertainty of waiting for divine action is well expressed there, but the hope for sharing an other-worldly kingdom has yet to be fully developed. That would be done in later Christian literature. 2 Peter points the way forward to it in the teachers' eschatological scepticism and in the author's expression of the heavenly hope.

Nor is this comment about the *parousia* hope intended to deny that 2 Peter has abiding significance as a work of literature. Its value in the eschatological debate lies in the insistence that all Christian expressions of the future hope must have an ethical dimension. Perhaps also Christian theology has moved too far in the direction of a humanitarian liberalism and ignored the biblical theme of judgment. 2 Peter powerfully reminds readers that judgment has its part to play in the Christian eschatological tradition. The fact that 2 Peter restates Jude's position while adapting his language is an instance of the way in which its author regarded judgment as a constant theme. Most of all, however, 2 Peter draws attention to the fact that Christianity must take seriously what may prove to be the permanence of the existing order if it is to be a credible force in the world. The hope for sharing the divine nature devolved on readers the need to live out their lives with ethical conviction. The relation between ethics and eschatology must feature in all statements of the Christian future hope if this vision is to be preserved.

For Further Reading

The commentaries mentioned in the bibliography are important, notably those by Bauckham (1983) and Neyrey (1993). As noted earlier, the former is more detailed but the latter makes important use of social scientific methodology.

4
JUDE AND 2 PETER IN THE CONTEXT OF EARLY CHRISTIANITY

THIS GUIDE CONCLUDES by asking about the place which the letters occupy in early Christianity and what they reveal about the nature of the developing religion. These are questions that can be answered only approximately. Neither letter can be dated with precision, we do not know where they were sent, and we know considerably less about the situation of the Palestinian and Roman churches where they came from than we would like. 2 Peter in particular has been the subject of dispute since Käsemann's essay (1964) relegated it to the mid-second century CE and commented on its supposedly 'primitive Catholic' attitude towards the Gnostic heretics. Study of some wider issues helps to set the two texts in perspective and comments on their significance as sources for early Christianity.

The Early Christian Eschatological Hope

The two letters cast much light on the nature of primitive Christian eschatological hopes. The fact that the two are often read together and the recognition that 2 Peter uses Jude as a source makes it possible to see whether, and if so, how eschatological belief developed in the period between which they were written.

The origins of Christian eschatology lay in Jesus' preaching about the kingdom of God (cf. Mk 1.15). Judaism in the early Common Era had entertained a variety of eschatological hopes and it would be unwise to present these in an overly 'systematic' way. While many Jews expected that 'the Messiah' would come, there seems to have been no precise agreement about who the Messiah was and what he would do. This makes it wrong to say that that there was a fixed 'messianic concept' which Jesus then fulfilled. Jesus probably thought about himself as Messiah (cf. Mk 8.27-38) but this view was not held universally by his followers until after the resurrection.

Jesus was evidently possessed by the belief that he was the eschatological prophet of God whose mission was to proclaim the imminence of the divine kingdom. Although the story about Jesus in Lk. 4.1-30 suits that Evangelist's purposes, this is no reason for denying its historicity. This story tells how Jesus read the scroll of Isaiah 61 in the Nazareth synagogue and how he proclaimed that he himself had been uniquely gifted with the Spirit in order to fulfil Second Isaiah's eschatological programme. An important part of Jesus' message was his proclamation that God's kingdom was 'near' (Mk 1.15). The saying found in Mk 9.1, which has been mentioned already in the Guide, makes Jesus say that some of the original disciples would not taste death until they had witnessed the kingdom's powerful arrival. This saying was remembered when the Gospels were written some thirty or more years later and it was preserved in connection with the vision of the transformed Jesus ('the Transfiguration') which we have seen anticipated the *parousia* in early Christian usage. Jesus himself seems to have taken a relatively short-term view of the kingdom's arrival even if he accepted that there would be some kind of a delay before the end. He was a prophet of the imminent end who might have been disappointed had he lived to see how things turned out.

The belief that Jesus would return from heaven (generally called 'the *parousia* hope') was a feature of the very earliest Christianity. The earliest New Testament letter that we possess says that the Lord (by which Paul means Jesus) would come from heaven with the angels with the strong implication that he would carry out the work of judgment and then reign on earth (1 Thess. 3.13; cf. 2 Thess. 1.7). The origins of the early Christian *parousia* hope probably lie in the belief that Jesus' death had left something unfulfilled when it was seen in the light of Old Testament predictions about the glorious victory of God. The habit developed of reading Old Testament literature as predictions of what *Jesus* would do, so that the sense that something yet remained to be fulfilled was satisfied by the hope that *Jesus* would come from heaven to bring in the Kingdom.

Jude reveals how this future hope was understood in Palestinian Jewish Christianity. As with all the New Testament letters, we see there a particular situation and a projected response rather than literature that is devoid of a social setting. The situation was one where people had been teaching an ethical position which the author held wrong. He responded by presenting these teachers in the same terms as notorious biblical sinners and by emphasizing the theme of judgment. It would be wrong to assume either that this prediction of judgment was a special feature of this situation or that it was confined to Jude. The author responded in this way because judgment was an important part of the Christian eschatological tradition. This had stemmed from Jesus (cf. Mt. 10.15) and from John the Baptist before him (Mt. 3.10). Paul or a later follower could describe the future punishment of sinners in almost vindictive terms in 2 Thess. 1.5-10, and this passage should be examined to see the wider context in which Jude's eschatology was written.

Jude's contribution to the Christian eschatological tradition lies in his attempt to harness biblical material to describe the fate of contemporary sinners in a thoroughgoing way. An example of this is Jude 14 where the author refers *1 En.* 1.9 to the false teachers of his own day and assumes on the basis of that passage that these would be punished. Jude assumes that the punishment would take place when Jesus returned from heaven and he links this to the ethical call in the closing verses of the letter as if to warn people of the dangers which surrounded those who were tempted to follow the teachers.

2 Peter was written at a time when some had begun to question the belief that Jesus would return from heaven. It is important to make the point that the hope for future divine intervention and an earthly kingdom of God persisted in

mainstream Christian literature until well into the second century CE and even beyond it. The likelihood that the false teachers in this letter had an Epicurean base makes it difficult to say how far their views would have been shared by many people, although perhaps some Christian churches had people on their fringes who were more willing to raise questions than others who were committed to preserving a tradition of exchatology. This author's insistence that belief in the *parousia* was still valid (ch. 3) and his repetition of the statement about the thief in the night shows that the belief in sudden divine intervention was still regarded as important by the Roman church at the time.

The difference between Jude and 2 Peter is thus that the earlier document simply accepts that the *parousia* would happen (v. 4) while the later one finds it necessary to justify that belief at some length. The fact remains that 2 Peter attests the questioning of the Christian eschatological hope. This is an important historical observation. It reveals the need that was felt to rethink the eschatological basis of Christianity which did in fact happen as the religion progressed to maturity with the recognition that the apostolic age had passed.

The Identity of Jude's Opponents

This Guide has tentatively advanced the theory that Jude's opponents had a connection with the wandering prophetic tradition in early Christianity. Although this is not said explicitly in the text it would at least explain how the teachers could have gained an entry into the community and it may explain why the author should take pains to deny that they had the Spirit (v. 19). The evidence for this view may now be presented in more detail to justify the suggestion which has been advanced here.

Wandering prophecy had been a feature of Christianity from the very beginning. Jesus was a wandering teacher who travelled around Galilee and then from Galilee to Jerusalem. The book of Acts says that key figures like Peter and Paul similarly journeyed further afield. Perhaps the Christians learned something from the Cynics in adopting this kind of

4. Jude and 2 Peter in Context

lifestyle (see Downing 1988). Collins is surely right to say that the motives for adopting a wandering lifestyle were varied in the emerging religion (1984: 135). One important reason may have been the desire to imitate Jesus himself which created a missionary fervour in view of the imminent end. It was to wandering prophets of this kind that some of the sayings in the Synoptic Gospels were apparently addressed; notably perhaps the saying about the Son of Man having nowhere to lay his head (Matt. 8.20), and probably that about those who left family and friends as well (Luke 18.29-30).

Problems sometimes arose with wandering prophets (see Collins 1984: 135-36). Some of these problems can be discerned from Matthew's Gospel. Mt. 7.15-16 warns against false prophets who appeared in sheeps' clothing but inside were ravenous wolves. The fact that they 'came' to a community emphasizes the itinerant nature of their ministry and their ability to gain an entrance from outside. Mt. 10.8b reminds of the need to give without pay, which is perhaps to be understood against a background where some prophets were charging for their services. The same Gospel lays down rules for the support of genuine prophets. Mt. 10.41 says that the person who received a prophet because he was a prophet would receive a prophet's reward (whatever that was).

Further information about the activity of wandering prophets is provided by the late first-century Syrian text called the *Didache*. The author of the *Didache* writes against a background where prophets were held in high esteem (11.7; 13.3-4) and where readers needed reminding not to despise the institutional leaders, who are said to 'exercise the ministry of the prophets' among them (15.1-2). This suggests a situation where the bishops and deacons had to fight for their authority in view of the respect accorded prophets at the time. The *Didache* also says that it was sinful to test any prophet when he was speaking in the Spirit (ch. 11), and that a prophet—but no one else—could give thanks in the Eucharistic Prayer using a free form of words. Besides upholding genuine prophecy the *Didache* supplies rules for discerning false prophets. Chapter 11 resembles some of the material in Matthew in specifying criteria through which these could be unmasked. Any prophet who stayed more than two days, who asked for money, or showed other forms of undesirable behaviour proved himself a false prophet. This is not just theoretical proscription but it no doubt reflects actual experience of sponging in which the duty of hospitality had been abused by wandering figures. As in Matthew, the criterion supplied for unmasking false prophets presupposes that they were able to gain entrance to a community simply on the grounds of being prophets. Their true or false status was revealed only later through their behaviour. Nothing is said in the *Didache* to indicate how false prophets should be removed once unmasked. Presumably this was done through ostracism, censure, or even straightforward ejection and the mind of the whole community would have been important in this. Genuine prophets needed no such measures for the over-riding criterion of their authenticity was the fact that they moved on without being asked to do so.

This material provides a possible background for the comment in Jude 4 that the teachers had gained access to the community and received an audience there. Were they perhaps wandering prophets who had been received as such by the church in question? The report about their behaviour at the *agape* (v. 12) indicates that hospitality was being abused and this can also be compared with the wider material. True prophets would neither have put their own interests before others', least of all at the fellowship meal, nor would they have stayed long enough for such behaviour to have become a community scandal. The fact that these people had failed to move on may have led some in the church to send word to the author and to ask for instructions about what to do about them. Perhaps the teachers were still there because others had found elements of their message attractive and they were encouraged to stay longer in defiance of the normal rules. The hints in Jude that they were interested in money and abused hospitality can both be illustrated from Matthew and the *Didache* and both were perhaps natural temptations for people who relied on others for their support.

This theory cannot be proved and it does not necessarily reveal anything about what the teachers were saying. We should certainly not assume that wandering prophets offered uniform teaching as they journeyed from church to church. The opposite is more likely to be true. Since they claimed inspiration by the Spirit, many of their oracles may have been circumstantially determined. It is likely that there would even have been elements of contradiction in what was said by different people. Not all people moved by the Spirit in early Christian churches were libertines. Some were ascetics (see *Asc. Isa.* 2.7-11) while many doubtless adopted the ethical position of Paul in Gal. 6.2, that freedom in Christ meant obedience to the law of Christ - a stance which is not far from what Jude himself says.

Were the Opponents in Either Letter 'Gnostics'?

Another issue that would benefit from clarification is the question of whether the opponents in either letter were 'Gnostics'. This hypothesis has been advanced in respect of both letters: of Jude's opponents by Sidebottom (1967: 69, 79) and of 2 Peter's by Käsemann (1964). Matters of dating and content tell against this hypothesis. The teachers in both cases may well have been libertines or antinomians, and have questioned ethics as well as eschatology, but we can hardly now call them Gnostics, given what we know about Gnosticism.

Gnosticism was a second-century complex of religions which taught an anthropological pessimism supported by a mythological cosmogony (for an introduction see Rudolph 1983). Gnostics debased the value of human life and sought to compensate for what they saw as its irrelevance by suggesting that the human condition had arisen through rebellion among the aeons, as a result of which fallen light particles had become imprisoned in human bodies. Cosmological and anthropological dualism lay at the heart of Gnosticism. The Gnostic's aim was to acquire *gnosis* (knowledge) which would enable his soul to return to the heavenly world after death. An essential part of this *gnosis* was the need to circumvent the heavenly warders who tried to stop the soul from making its ascension. Gnostic pessimism about the value of human life issued in two contrasting attitudes:

there was both an ascetic and a libertine wing. Ascetics mortified the flesh, while libertines indulged it.

Those who believe that the opponents in Jude and 2 Peter were Gnostics argue that they were libertine Gnostics who gave vent to their passions under the belief that how you used your body when on earth mattered little when compared with the soul's heavenly destiny at death. The dating of Gnostic literature seriously compromises the suggestion that the opponents in either letter were 'Gnostics'. The Gnostic library which turned up in Nag Hammadi (Egypt) just after the Second World War (translation edited by Robinson 1988) contains documents that most scholars would not date before about 150 CE. Even if we allow that Gnosticism must have arisen over a period of time and that it had antecedents, not least in Jewish and Christian literature, we should beware of supposing that the full gamut of Gnostic ideas was known in the first century CE. The general consensus regarding the Fourth Gospel, which was for a long time felt to have been influenced by Gnostic ideas, is now that it represents a *step towards* Gnosticism and that the background of its christology lies in Jewish apocalyptic and not in the Gnostic Redeemer Myth.

We have to turn to second century literature to find more obvious steps towards Gnosticism. The *Ascension of Isaiah*, which was written in Syria perhaps between 112–138 CE, uses ideas that Gnostics would later take up, including the words of the Demiurge 'I alone am' (4.6) but significantly in a different way (on this text see Knight 1995). The *Ascension of Isaiah* lacks the thoroughgoing cosmic dualism of the Gnostic literature and it firmly excludes the demon Beliar from the heavens so that God had no rival there. The *Ascension of Isaiah* seems more obviously 'Gnosticizing' than the Fourth Gospel with its account of the Saviour's descent (chs. 10 and 11) and notion of the heavenly warders (10.17-31). To speak, as we must do, of *differences* between this apocalypse and Gnosticism confirms that first-century literature like Jude and 2 Peter ought to be distinguished from Gnosticism as well. Neither letter reveals a cosmological dualism nor any cosmogonic interest which were essential ingredients of Gnosticism. As was noted, Neyrey has now in any event proposed the much more convincing thesis that the opponents in 2 Peter, far from being Gnostics, had some kind of contact with Epicureanism. The 'Gnostic' hypothesis would not now perhaps claim many supporters

Jude, 2 Peter and 'Early Catholicism'

Another issue that is often discussed with regard to this literature is the problem of whether the two letters, and especially 2 Peter, enshrine what has been called an 'early catholicism'. That term is a loose one and it seems to mean a number of different things according to which scholar is using it. Broadly speaking 'early catholicism' draws a contrast between the initial years of the Christian movement, which were characterized by a freedom of worship and by Spirit-filled activity, and the appearance of a more routine pattern of church life, often associated with the writings of Clement (96 CE) and Ignatius (110 CE) in the immediate post-apostolic period. Clearly, it is impossible to be precise about when this shift took place. Like many historical movements it can be discerned only in retrospect, and then on a broad scale. The paucity of evidence makes it difficult to see the change in progress. In many ways the middle of the second century, round about the time of the initial Gnostic controversy, is a better marker for speaking about 'early catholicism' for it was only then that the church had to confront a full scale 'heretical' movement and it began to examine its traditions and beliefs in detail in order to resolve the issue.

This observation begs the question of whether Jude and 2 Peter display 'early catholic' tendencies and what it might suggest if they do. This question as it is put to the literature has often been one of dating: the fact that either is felt to display 'early catholic' features has been used as an argument that they were written beyond the apostolic period. This in turn supports the belief that they display a different kind of Christianity from that found in the letters of Paul. For those who want to do so, like Käsemann, this can then be used to argue that their evidence is less important than that of other New Testament documents.

This line of argument must not be allowed to validate the

suggestion that change happens according to a strict chronological sequence. We have evidence of the crystallization of faith into set formulae as early as Paul (Col. 1.15-16; Phil. 2.5-11) who found it helpful to incorporate existing christological statements in his letters. Philippians is an interesting letter because it mentions the *parousia* hope only in several passing references and it also alludes to 'bishops and deacons' evidently as ministers in the church at Philippi (1.1). Thus several of the characteristics which have often been held to display 'early catholicism' are found in the letters of Paul whose literary career ended some thirty years after the resurrection of Jesus.

It is helpful in this respect to distinguish between Jude and 2 Peter in terms of the authority which the two authors claim for their opinions. Jude writes as the brother of James. The authorities that he cites are the Old Testament and the words of the apostles. 2 Peter also claims the apostles as authorities, but the fact that the author specifically names Peter and Paul, and draws on Jude as well, suggests that his letter comes from a later period when the need to find authentication by appealing to the original figures was paramount. As opposed to the author of Jude, the writer of 2 Peter goes to such lengths to claim apostolic authority that it seems that many of the apostles must have been dead when he wrote. This shift in the understanding of authority does seem to be an important feature of what might and ought to be called 'early catholicism'. This was bound up with the recognition that those who had been commissioned by Jesus enjoyed a position of prominence that a later generation could imitate but never replace. This sense of distance from the apostles distinguishes 2 Peter from Jude but it is conceivable that 2 Peter was written when some of the original generation were still alive. The shift towards 'early catholicism' is one which demonstrates a respect for earlier literature and this, as well as the recognition that key apostles were dead, must be acknowledged in further discussion of the subject.

The Authors as Interpreters Again

Two further points deserve to be made about the way in which Jude and 2 Peter make use of earlier literature. The first is the form in which they choose to do this, that of the catena of biblical allusions, and the second the rationale which permitted Scripture to be interpreted in this way.

The device of presenting a catena of scriptural citations or allusions is found also in the literature of the Qumran community and it was not distinctively Christian either in origin or in usage. It can be paralleled in works such as the Qumran *Messianic Anthology* and in Christian literature in passages like Romans 9–11. Jude shows how a Christian author took up a catena of references, not all of them from the Bible, with which he knew that his readers were familiar and how he used them with cumulative effect to make a point about a situation in his own day. What unites all his incidents together is the fact that they describe notorious incidents of rebellion from Israel's history which resulted in punishment. It is significant that his major proof text for the *parousia* is taken not from the Bible but from 1 En. 1.9. While this should not be taken as evidence that Jude regarded *1 Enoch* as 'canonical'—it is anachronistic to use that term of Jewish literature in this context of interpretation—it nevertheless shows the high regard in which Christians held Jewish apocalyptic literature and illustrates their tendency to see all references to 'the Lord' visiting the earth for judgment as prophecies of the parousia.

The hermeneutical method which Jude employs is that of typology. That is to say, he saw all the incidents as referring to the false teachers of his own day. This implies the view that the original writers had not been able to see the full implications of what they were writing. The method bears comparison with information found in the Qumran *Habakkuk Commentary* (1QpHab) whose author said that God told the prophet what would happen in the last age but not when time would come to an end, and with Paul in 1 Cor. 10.11 who interprets the punishment following the wilderness murmuring as an example that had been recorded for his own readers' benefit. Paul agrees with the Qumran author that such interpretation was possible because the 'end of the ages' had arrived. Christianity thus shared with the Qumran community the tendency to see Scripture as reinforcing its sectarian consciousness which rested on deep eschatological convictions.

For Further Reading

The effect of the *parousia* hope on New Testament literature is examined by A.L. Moore, *The Parousia in the New Testament* (Leiden: Brill, 1966). The nature of 'early catholicism' has been examined by J.D.G. Dunn in his *Unity and Diversity in the New Testament* (London: SCM Press, 1977), pp. 341-66. M. Hengel has significantly shown that the phrase 'early catholicism' might describe the religious outlook of Jesus and Paul; *Acts and the History of Early Christianity* (ET; London: SCM Press, 1979), p. 122.

Bibliography

Here is a list of the works mentioned in the text, together with some suggestions for further reading. In the text of the Guide, I have referred to all literature by author and date only (with 'a' and 'b' as explained in square '[]' brackets). Each chapter concludes with a review of the relevant secondary literature.

1. *Commentaries on the Letters*
Bauckham, R.J., *Jude, 2 Peter* (Waco, TX: Word Books, 1983).
—*Jude, 2 Peter* (Dallas: Word Books, 1990) [Bauckham, 1990a].
Bigg, C., *A Critical and Exegetical Commentary on the Epistles of St Peter and St Jude* (Edinburgh: T. & T. Clark, 1901).
Cranfield, C.E.B., *1 & 2 Peter and Jude* (London: SCM Press, 1960).
Kelly, J.N.D., *A Commentary on the Epistles of Peter and Jude* (London: A. & C. Black, 1969).
Neyrey, J.H., *2 Peter, Jude: A New Translation with Introduction and Commentary* (AB, 37c; New York: Doubleday, 1993).
Reicke, B, *The Epistles of James, Peter, and Jude: Introduction, Translation and Notes* (AB, 37; New York: Doubleday, 1964).
Sidebottom, E.M., *James, Jude and 2 Peter* (NCB; London: Nelson, 1967).
Spitta, F., *Der zweite Brief des Petrus und der Brief des Judas* (Halle, 1885).

2. *Other studies mentioned in my text*
Baltzer, K., *The Covenant Formulary in Old Testament, Jewish and Early Christian Writings* (Oxford: Basil Blackwell, 1971).
Bauckham, R.J., *Jude and the Relatives of Jesus in the Early Church* (Edinburgh: T. & T. Clark, 1990) [Bauckham, 1990b].
Bietenhard, H., 'The Millennial Hope in the Early Church', *SJT* 6 (1953), pp. 12-30.
Birdsall, J.N., 'The Text of Jude in P[72]', *JTS* 14 (1963), pp. 394-99
Charles, J.D., *Literary Strategy in the Epistle of Jude* (London and Toronto: Associated University Presses, 1993).
Chester, A., and R.P. Martin, *The Theology of the Letters of James,*

Peter and Jude (Cambridge: Cambridge University Press, 1994).
Collins, A.Y., *Crisis and Catharsis: the Power of the Apocalypse* (Philadelphia: Westminster Press, 1984).
Cullmann, O., *Peter: Disciple, Apostle, Martyr* (ET; London: SCM Press, 2nd edn, 1962).
Downing, F.G., *Christ and the Cynics* (Sheffield: JSOT Press, 1988).
Dunn, J.D.G., *Unity and Diversity in the New Testament* (London: SCM Press, 1977).
Fornberg, T., *The Early Church in a Pluralistic Society: A Study of 2 Peter* (Lund: Gleerup, 1977).
Guthrie, D., *New Testament Introduction* (Leicester: Apollos Press, 4th edn, 1990).
Hengel, M., *Acts and the History of Early Christianity* (ET; London: SCM Press, 1979).
Käsemann, E., 'An Apologia for Primitive Christian Eschatology', in his *Essays on New Testament Themes* (ET; SBT, 41; London: SCM Press, 1964), pp. 169-95.
Knight, J.M., *The Ascension of Isaiah* (Sheffield: JSOT Press, 1995).
Kolenkow, A., 'The Genre Testament and Forecasts of the Future in the Hellenistic Jewish Milieu', *JSJ* 6 (1975), pp. 57-71.
Lossky, V., *The Mystical Theology of the Eastern Church* (Cambridge: Clarke, 1957).
Moore, A.L., *The Parousia in the New Testament* (Leiden: Brill, 1966).
Neyrey, J.H., 'The Form and Background of the Polemic in 2 Peter', *JBL* 99 (1980), pp. 407-31.
Osburn, C.D., 'The Text of Jude 22-23', *ZNW* 63 (1972), pp. 139-44.
Robinson, J.A.T., *Redating the New Testament* (London: SCM Press, 1976).
Robinson, J.M. (ed.), *The Nag Hammadi Library in English* (Leiden: Brill, 3rd edn, 1988).
Rudolph, K., *Gnosis, the Nature and History of an Ancient Religion* (ET; Edinburgh: T. & T. Clark, 1983).
Thiede, C., *Simon Peter: from Galilee to Rome* (Exeter: Paternoster Press, 1986).
Vermes, G., *Post-Biblical Jewish Studies* (Leiden: Brill, 1975).

3. *The letter form in early Christianity*

Aune, D.E., *The New Testament in its Literary Environment* (Philadelphia: Westminster Press, 1987).
Doty, W.G., *Letters in Primitive Christianity* (Philadelphia: Fortress Press, 1973).
Roetzel, C., *The Letters of Paul: Conversations in Context* (Louisville, KY: Westminster/John Knox Press, 3rd edn, 1991).

White, J.L., *The Form and Function of the Body of the Greek Letter: A Study of the Letter-Body in the Non-Literary Papyri and in Paul the Apostle* (SBLDS, 2; Missoula, MT: Scholars Press, 1972).

4. *Prophecy in Early Christianity*
Aune, D.E., *Prophecy in Early Christianity and the Ancient Mediterranean World* (Grand Rapids: Eerdmans, 1983).
Hill, D., *New Testament Prophecy* (London: Marshalls, 1979).

INDEXES

INDEX OF REFERENCES

Old Testament		95.8	49	7.15-16	79
Genesis		105.42	37	8.20	79
4.8	47			10.3	11
6	12, 34,	*Proverbs*		10.8	79
	44	9.7-8	51	10.15	77
6.1-3	43	15.6	51	10.41	79
6.4	43	25.14	49	11.21	46
6.5	43	26.11	66	12.43-45	66
19	44			12.45	18
19.5	44	*Isaiah*		16.18	58
		34.4	70	18.6	66
Exodus		41.9	38	23	46
2.12	45	57.20	49	24.43	19, 69
		61	76	28.18-20	58
Leviticus		65.17	70		
21.21	65			*Mark*	
		Ezekiel		1.15	75, 76
Numbers		34	48	1.16	58
14	34, 42			1.19	24
14.2	49	*Daniel*		3.18	24
15.37-41	47	11.36	50	6.3	25
16	47	12.3	59	8.27-38	76
16.1-2	47			8.29	58
22–24	47	*Amos*		9.1-8	17
24.17	62	6.1	46	9.1	18, 68,
25	47				76
26	42	*Habakkuk*		9.20	24
		2.3	69	10.37	24
Deuteronomy				10.45	37
13	29, 44	*Zechariah*		12.6	38
19.15	34	3.2	14, 54		
26.8	42	3.3-4	53	*Luke*	
34.6	46	14.5	49	4.1-30	76
				9.31	42
Nehemiah		*Wisdom of Solomon*		11.24-26	66
9.14	37	2.23	60	18.29-30	79
				20.36	59
Psalms		New Testament			
35	51	*Matthew*		*John*	
38.16	54	3.10	77	1.17	59
90.4	19, 69	7.7-17	49	3.16	38

8.28	38	2.2	24	1.7	22
8.58	43	2.4	41	1.9	22
12.41	43	2.8	57	1.13	22
		2.11-14	11, 58	2.6	22
Acts		2.12	24, 41	3.20	63
2.2	24	3.19	45	3.30	23
5.31	25	4.21-31	30		
6.1	51	5.13	12	*2 Peter*	
9.11	25	5.16	41	1.1	22, 58
10	58	5.22	39, 60	1.2	58
12.17	11, 24	6.2	30, 81	1.3-11	16, 59
13	33			1.3-4	16, 59
15	30	*Ephesians*		1.4	59, 61, 66
15.13-21	11	2.20	57, 67		
15.15	24	5.3	45	1.5-8	16
15.22	25	5.27	70	1.5-7	60
15.26	25	6.21-22	20	1.9	16
20.29-30	50			1.10-11	61
		Philippians		1.10	16
Romans		1.1	84	1.11	16, 23, 61
1.1	37	2.5-11	37, 84		
1.6-7	38	2.7	37	1.12-18	16, 22, 23, 63
4.3	16				
8.9	51	*Colossians*		1.12-15	61
8.18-25	70	1.15-16	84	1.12	61
8.21	70	1.20	59	1.14	61
9–11	85	2.15	64	1.15	16, 61
10.6	64	4.7-8	20	1.16-18	15, 16, 35, 61, 67
12	52				
		1 Thessalonians			
1 Corinthians		3.13	43, 49, 76	1.16	61
3.3-4	51			1.19-21	17, 35, 61, 63
3.10-17	52	4.13-18	68		
6.12	12	5.2	69	1.19	62, 67
8	30	5.6-11	70	1.20-21	62
10.4	43			1.20	62
10.7-11	42	*2 Thessalonians*		2	17, 59, 62, 63, 66
10.11	13, 85	1.5-10	77		
11.10	45	1.7	49, 76		
11.17-22	48			2.1-18	20
12–14	30	*2 Timothy*		2.1-2	16
12	52	3.1-5	50	2.1	17, 35, 63
12.28	57, 67				
13	60	*Hebrews*		2.3-18	21
15	68	2.2	45	2.3	63
15.7	24, 58	3–4	42	2.4-10	63
15.44	51			2.4-9	63
		James		2.4	17, 31, 63
2 Corinthians		1.1	25, 37, 38		
3.7-18	30	2.24	56	2.5	17, 20, 21, 23, 63, 69
5	68				
		1 Peter			
Galatians		1.1-2	23	2.6	17, 63, 69
1.15-17	58	1.1	71		

2.7-8	17, 20, 64	3.15-16	33, 35, 63	14-15	14
2.7	63	3.15	19, 70	14	13, 43, 44, 49, 77
2.9	64	3.16	19, 71		
2.10-22	17	3.17	20	16-18	20
2.10-18	21	3.18	20, 71	16	14, 65, 66
2.10-11	17, 64	4.16	71		
2.10a	64			17-23	12, 50
2.12	17, 64-66	*Jude*		17-19	42
2.13	17, 64, 70	1-2	11	17-18	14, 28
		1	11, 12, 23, 24, 37-39	17	50, 67
2.14	17, 33, 65			19	14, 28, 30, 51, 52, 78
2.15-16	15, 18	2	39		
2.15	17, 65	3-23	11	20-23	21, 52
2.16	65, 66	3-4	12	20	14
2.17-18	18	3	26, 39, 40, 50	21	14, 34, 52, 53
2.17	18, 65				
2.18	18, 65	4-18	21	22-23	14, 53
2.19	18, 66	4-13	20	22	14
2.20	18, 66	4	12, 28, 29, 41, 52, 63, 78, 80	23	14, 53
2.21	18, 66			24-25	11, 14, 54
2.22	18				
3	15, 18, 19, 59, 60, 67, 78	5-19	42	24	38
		5-16	42	*Revelation*	
		5-7	34	1.3	55
3.1-3	20	5	12, 41, 42	3.3	69
3.1-2	22, 23, 67			21.1	19, 70
		6	12, 43, 44, 46, 63	*Pseudepigrapha*	
3.1	18, 23, 35, 67, 71			*Ahiqar*	
		7	12, 34, 44, 63	8.18	66
3.2	67			*Asc. Isa.*	
3.3-13	73	8-10	64	2.7-11	81
3.3-4	18	8-9	28, 29	3.21-31	50
3.3	50, 67	8	13, 29, 44, 50	3.21	50, 68
3.4	15, 18, 22, 28, 33, 50, 68	9	13, 45, 64	4.3	16
				4.6	82
		10	13, 46, 51	4.13	50, 68
3.5-6	19, 69			4.18	69, 70
3.7	69	11	13, 15, 18, 20, 21, 28, 46, 47, 65	10	82
3.8-10	69			10.7-31	82
3.8	19			11	82
3.9	19				
3.10	19, 22, 69		65	*1 Enoch*	
		12-13	12, 13, 48, 49, 55, 65, 80	1.6-9	69
3.11-12	19	12		1.9	13, 14, 49, 77, 85
3.11	70, 72				
3.12	19, 22, 70			5.4	50
3.13	19, 70	13	13, 49, 65	6-19	43
3.14	70			7	43

Index of References

8	43	Qumran		*Apostolic Constitutions*	
10.12	44	*CD*		7.46	25
16.3	43	4.4	38		
18.13-16	49			*Didache*	
45.4-5	70	Targums		11	29, 79
86.1-6	49	*Pal. Targ.*		11.7	79
101.3	50	4.8	15	13.3-4	79

2 Enoch
22.7   45

Jubilees
1.29   70

3 Maccabbees
2.4   63

Ps. Philo
16.1   47
18.13   47

Sib. Or.
2.187-213 69

T. Mos.
5.5   50

T. Naph.
3.5   63

Philo
Quaest. in Exod.
2.29   60

Vit. Mos.
1.266-68 47

Josephus
Ant.
1.52-66   47
1.194   44

Christian Authors
1 Clem.
23   28
23.3   68
5.4   16
23   18, 32

2 Clem.
11.2   68

Eusebius
Hist.Eccl.
3.19.1-3.20.7 25
4.22.4   24

Herm. Sim.
9.17.5   66

Jerome
Ep.
120.11   22

Justin
1 Apology
20.1-2   69

INDEX OF AUTHORS

Aune, D.E. 88, 89

Baltzer, K. 59, 87
Bauckham, R.J. 20, 21, 24-26, 28, 35, 45, 47, 53, 56, 60, 61, 63, 64, 68, 69, 74, 87
Bietenhard, H. 69, 87
Bigg, C. 21, 87
Birdsall, J.N. 53, 87

Charles, J.D. 11, 33, 34, 38, 40, 56, 87
Chester, A. 36, 87
Collins, A.Y. 79, 88
Cranfield, C.E.B. 21, 36, 87
Cullmann, O. 58, 88

Doty, W.G. 38, 88
Downing, F.G. 79, 88
Dunn, J.D.G. 86, 88

Fornberg, T. 21, 36, 88

Guthrie, D. 22, 88

Hengel, M. 86, 88
Hill, D. 89

Käsemann, E. 27, 75, 81, 83, 88
Kelly, J.N.D. 21, 23, 36, 53, 87

Knight, J.M. 82, 88
Kolenkow, A. 16, 88

Lossky, V. 60, 88

Martin, R.P. 36, 87
Moore, A.L. 86, 88

Neyrey, J.H. 15, 21, 27, 31, 35, 56, 66, 67, 74, 87, 88

Osburn, C.D. 53, 88

Reicke, B. 21, 87
Robinson, J.A.T. 88
Robinson, J.M. 20, 82, 88
Roetzel, C. 38, 88
Rudolph, K. 81, 88

Sidebottom, E.M. 31, 81, 87
Spitta, F. 21, 87

Thiede, C. 58, 88

Vermes, G. 47, 88

White, J.L. 89
Wilson, W.E. 69